Barbara Ellis, Editor
Frances Tenenbaum, Series Editor

HOUGHTON MIFFLIN COMPANY
Boston • New York

Water Gardens

CHARLES B. THOMAS

How to Plan and Plant a Backyard Pond

For information about permission to reproduce selections from this book,
write to Permissions, Houghton Mifflin Company, 215 Park Avenue South,
New York, New York 10003.

For information about this and other Houghton Mifflin trade
and reference books and multimedia products, visit The Bookstore at
Houghton Mifflin on the World Wide Web at http://www.hmco.com/trade/.

Taylor's Guide is a registered trademark of Houghton Mifflin Company.

Library of Congress Cataloging-in-Publication Data

Thomas, Charles B. (Charles Brosius), date.
    Water gardens : how to plan and plant a backyard pond / Charles
Thomas ; [Barbara Ellis, editor].
       p.   cm. — (Taylor's weekend gardening guides ; 5)
    Includes bibliographical references and index.
    ISBN 0-395-81590-8
    1. Water gardens. I. Ellis, Barbara W. II. Title. III. Series.
    SB423.T455 1997
    635.9'674—dc21   97-10468

Printed in the United States of America.

WCT 10 9 8 7 6 5 4 3 2

Book design by Deborah Fillion
Cover photograph © by Lilypons Water Gardens

Contents

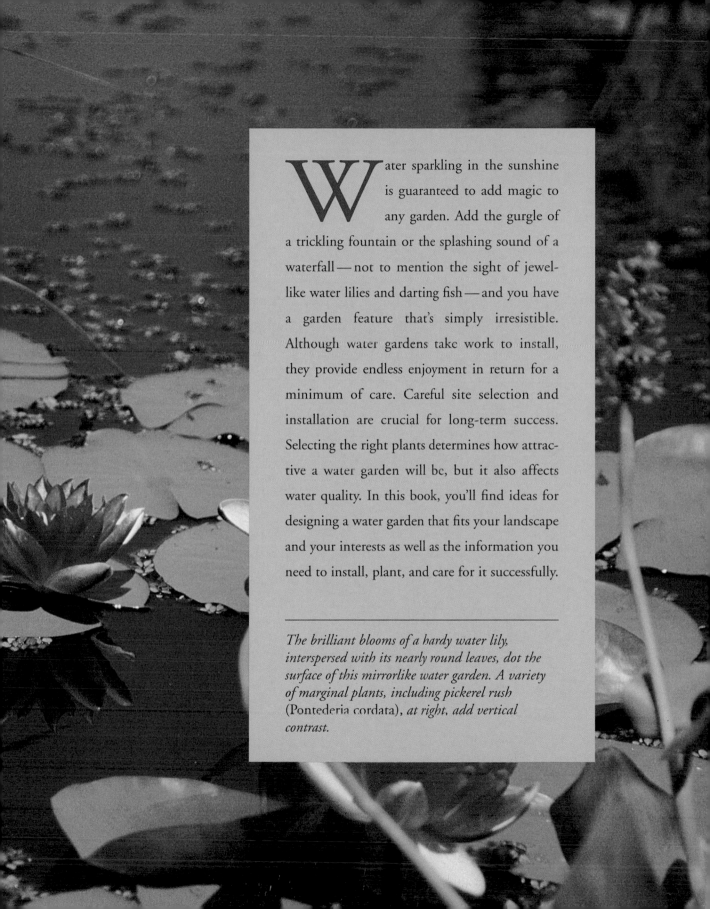

Water sparkling in the sunshine is guaranteed to add magic to any garden. Add the gurgle of a trickling fountain or the splashing sound of a waterfall — not to mention the sight of jewel-like water lilies and darting fish — and you have a garden feature that's simply irresistible. Although water gardens take work to install, they provide endless enjoyment in return for a minimum of care. Careful site selection and installation are crucial for long-term success. Selecting the right plants determines how attractive a water garden will be, but it also affects water quality. In this book, you'll find ideas for designing a water garden that fits your landscape and your interests as well as the information you need to install, plant, and care for it successfully.

The brilliant blooms of a hardy water lily, interspersed with its nearly round leaves, dot the surface of this mirrorlike water garden. A variety of marginal plants, including pickerel rush (Pontederia cordata), *at right, add vertical contrast.*

Chapter 1:

Planning a Water Garden

M ost gardeners don't list planning among their favorite activities. Getting out into the garden to move soil around or fill a bed with flowers is simply much more appealing. When it comes to installing a water garden, however, good planning pays long-term dividends. Careful site selection is an all-important first step. In the right site, a water garden can be nearly maintenance-free, but a pool plopped in the backyard without much thought can mean unending headaches and disappointment. Before getting too far into the planning process, it's also important to check local regulations regarding pools and other bodies of water. In some areas, pools over a certain depth must be fenced.

A well-planned water garden can also become the focal point that transforms an ordinary backyard into something really special. You can use it to unify the overall design of your landscape, enhance an existing flower bed or shrub border, create a quiet oasis where the world seems far away, or accent a patio or deck to create an irresistible area for sitting or entertaining. Surprisingly enough, a water

Water adds appeal to any garden, and there is a style and size pool for every property. A freeform pond like this one makes a spectacular accent in the center of a large lawn, but a pool with a simple fountain adds charm to even the tiniest garden nook.

garden also can be the perfect solution for a site where you have trouble growing anything because of poor soil conditions. Whether your garden is a tiny courtyard or rooftop, a sprawling suburban lot or country place, there is a way effectively to incorporate the sight and sound of water.

SELECTING THE PERFECT SITE

Start your quest for the perfect site by determining which parts of your yard receive the most sunshine. In order to bloom well, water lilies require a *minimum* of 5 to 6 hours of direct sun daily — 8 hours is even better. Although there are lilies that bloom with as little as 2 hours of sun daily, all bloom best in full sun.

A map of your property, drawn to scale, will help you plan. Use it to keep notes about sun and shade patterns, surface water drainage areas, and other features, as well as to experiment with water garden shapes and sizes. Start with a map of your property drawn to scale on graph paper. Suit the scale to the size of your yard, and make the map as large as possible so you'll have plenty of room to write. A scale of one square equals one foot works fine for small gardens; use a scale such as one square equals two or even five feet for larger properties.

Use a survey of your property, if you have one, to determine its dimensions. Otherwise, use a tape measure or string marked off at 10-foot intervals and ask a friend to help you measure. Once you have marked the boundaries on the map, indicate north and write down the scale as well. Then draw in the house, garage, and other buildings to scale. Write in all the mature trees on the map next, and draw a dotted line around each trunk to indicate the full spread of its branches, or canopy. (Mark the estimated canopy *at maturity* for young trees.) Mark the location of any buried electrical cables, gas lines, or cable TV lines. Finally, draw in existing flower beds, shrub borders, patios, decks, and other features. This is your base map.

To avoid the need to draw and redraw your base map as you design, cover it with large sheets of tracing paper as overlays. Each time you start a new overlay, trace a few key points from the base map onto it so it is easy to line up with the base map. (The corners of your property work well for this.) You can draw on overlays any way you like, experimenting with shapes and sizes of pools. Use one color or many, and combine sketched shapes with notes if you like. When

Good site selection and thoughtful design are the keys to a successful water garden. The flagstone bridge across this pond accomplishes a dual purpose: It makes it easy to get from one side of the garden to the other, and it also lets visitors stand directly over the water to peer into its depths.

one overlay gets too messy, simply place another overlay on top of it, trace the features you want to keep, and discard the old one.

On the first overlay, use pencil to draw in areas that are shady—hatch marks or circles are fine. Look at your yard in the morning, at noon, and later in the afternoon and draw in the patterns of shade cast by trees and buildings at each time of day. (These patterns change from day to day through the year, so you may want to record them in spring, early summer, summer, and fall.) Sun and shade patterns alone may determine the best site for a water garden, but there are other factors to consider when choosing a site. You can make separate overlays for each of the following factors or combine your notes onto a single master plan.

View from the House. A water garden can provide considerable enjoyment from indoors if you take time to site it properly. Take your base map from room to room and note which sites will be visible from key windows. Being able to see even a corner of a water garden from the kitchen window will help make washing dishes more enjoyable, for example. Siting a water garden so it is framed in the French doors off the living room can create a spectacular view.

Outdoor Living Areas. Once a water garden is filled with fish and plants, it draws people like a magnet. Everyone in your household will want to check daily to see what's in bloom or visit with a favorite fish. Visitors will be drawn to it, too. Dinner guests and delivery people alike will want to stand at its edge, ask questions, and peer down into its depths. Select a site and plan the surroundings accordingly. A site adjacent to a deck or patio is ideal because it provides a comfortable spot from which to enjoy the water and its inhabitants. Locating the water garden away from the house creates a destination in the yard—a feature that draws people out into the garden. Be sure to plan the water garden so visitors can walk up close to the edge; they'll find it frustrating to be separated from the water's edge by broad flower beds or other obstructions. A comfortable garden seat nearby provides a place to sit quietly, read a book, and enjoy the show.

Traffic Patterns. A water garden makes a wonderful feature to entice people out into the yard. Consider siting yours as part of an overall plan designed to draw visitors out the back door and through the garden. Avoid siting a water garden

Although a deck and water garden combination like this one requires special skills to design and build, it obviously provides an appealing perch from which to enjoy the water. A heavily planted slope behind the garden provides privacy and an attractive setting for a waterfall.

smack in the middle of a utilitarian path, however, such as the one out to the garage or between the driveway and the vegetable garden. In such sites, it may become an annoying obstacle. If there are no other choices, plan a bridge. Sites on the edge of or in the middle of the kids' playground pose their own set of problems and are best avoided as well.

Topography and Runoff. Although common sense would seem to dictate that a low-lying area that collects water might be a good choice for a water garden, in this case, common sense is wrong. Runoff during a rainstorm could fill a pond with mud and debris as well as pesticide and fertilizer residues — even if you don't use them, they can come from a neighbor's garden. For best results, select a level

This rectangular garden makes the most of a difficult site, bounded by trees and a building on one side and a grade change in the foreground. The simple shape, echoed by a narrow bed of perennials and annuals alongside the building, transforms an otherwise awkward space into an appealing terrace.

site that does not collect water. If your best site would be difficult to level or is subject to runoff, or if you suspect a high water table, large boulders, or other obstacles underground, see "Dealing with Problem Sites" on page 30. "Water-falls" on page 16 offers another option for dealing with a sloping site.

Existing Ponds, Streams, and Springs. If any of these features exist on your property, consult local wetland authorities before making plans to modify them. Diverting water from a spring or stream to create a new pond, or enlarging a stream to form a pond, may require a permit from local authorities. This book focuses primarily on water gardens that are created artificially with a preformed fiberglass pool or a flexible liner. For a variety of reasons, liners don't work well when used with natural water sources. You definitely want the advice of an expert before you modify an existing pond, stream, or spring—better yet, have an expert do the installation for you.

Many of the plants in chapter 4 can be planted along the edges of an existing pond or stream or in the damp soil at the base of a spring to create a spectacular bog garden. Choose water lilies and marginal plants that stay in clumps and do not spread vigorously to avoid unintended takeover in and around natural, earth-bottomed ponds.

Existing Plantings. These can enhance a water garden or cause unending headaches, depending on the site you select. Keep water gardens well away from trees. Not only will falling leaves clog the water in autumn, but the outstretched roots of trees might also damage flexible pond liners, causing the pond to leak. They also may heave fiberglass liners out of the ground. To minimize the effect of large trees and shrubs, refer to your sun-and-shade-pattern overlay and select a site that is not shaded by trees at any time during the day. Refer to "Dealing with Problem Sites" on page 30 if your yard does not offer a full-sun site.

Existing plantings can create a stunning setting for a water garden, or you can design new flower beds or shrub borders for this purpose. Consider nestling a water garden next to a flower bed so the blooms will be reflected in the water on sunny days. Plantings of small trees and shrubs can provide an attractive backdrop for a water garden, too, adding texture and color to the garden, casting reflections, and creating a natural-looking setting. Use backdrops to hide an unattractive view that might detract from your water garden. Cover a fence with flowering vines such as clematis to form a colorful backdrop without sacrificing space in a small garden. For best results, plan on a wide swath of low ground covers or grass between trees and shrubs and the water garden to keep shade off the surface and leaves out of the water.

Electricity and Water. Plan on having access to electricity at the site you select to operate a pump for a filter, fountain, or waterfall. Although not essential to success, these features help keep the water clear and full of oxygen. Just as important, moving water makes a garden much more appealing. Having a pump also makes it easy to drain the pond for cleaning. A nearby source of electricity also makes lighting the pond more convenient so you can enjoy it on summer

evenings. It's also necessary if you use an electric deicer in winter to keep the water from freezing. Be sure to use a circuit with a ground fault interrupter (GFI); for more on these and on using electric appliances around a water garden, see "Selecting Pumps, Filters, and Lighting" on page 48.

Easy access to water is another plus. Every water garden needs to be filled up or topped off from time to time; siting a water garden within easy reach of an outdoor faucet makes it easy to accomplish this using a garden hose.

DETERMINING SIZE, SHAPE, AND STYLE

Once you have settled on a potential site, the next step is to decide how large a water garden you want to have and what it will look like. Identify the selected site on an overlay over your base map. You may want to draw a new base map of the site, to a larger scale, to use for designing the size and shape of the garden as well as the plantings and other features around it.

Size. Surprisingly, when it comes to water gardening, starting small is not always the best way to get one's feet wet. A garden in a half-barrel or other small container may seem like a good first test of whether you will be successful with a water garden, but it isn't necessarily. In-ground water gardens are much easier to manage than on-the-patio container gardens, and larger gardens often are easier than smaller ones. That's because temperature fluctuation in above-ground pools is greater than in in-ground ones because of the insulating effect of the surrounding soil. Temperatures also fluctuate more in smaller pools than in larger ones. Temperature fluctuation stresses fish, scavengers, and plants, and interferes with having a healthy living community. Also, the loss of two or three living things may have a profoundly adverse effect on a small half-barrel community, while such a loss might have hardly any effect on a 100-square-foot pond. One remedy is to site small pools and container gardens so they receive shade during the hottest part of the day. This helps control the serious problem of too much heat increase during the day. In fact, water lilies in small, above-ground gardens bloom more if they receive a few hours of shade during the hottest part of the day. Otherwise, midday heat buildup stresses the plants, resulting in reduced flower production.

In above-ground water gardens, especially tiny ones like this barrel garden, it is important to minimize water temperature fluctuations. For this reason, a site that receives several hours of shade during the hottest part of the day is best. The water lily in this garden is diminutive 'Helvola'.

The best advice about size is to put in as large a water garden as you can afford and your site can comfortably accommodate. Gardeners bitten by the water-gardening bug inevitably want more space for water lilies and fish, not less. Adding additional water gardens is certainly an option, but one large, well-designed pond is usually more satisfying from a design standpoint than several smaller ones. If you can afford only a small pond but have dreams of installing a larger one in a year or two, design both now. Give the lion's share of your best site to the dreamed-of large garden, and locate the smaller garden adjacent to it. When the time comes to install the large garden, you'll have a number of options: You can leave both ponds side by side and meld them together with plantings; eliminate the smaller pond; turn the smaller pond into a bog garden; or connect the two with overlapping liners or a waterfall.

As you design the size and shape, also plan how you will access areas on all sides of the water garden. You'll need to be able to plant, weed, and mulch on all sides of it, so make sure your plan allows for easy access. Draw maintenance paths or stepping stones to make sure you can get to crucial areas.

Shape and Style. A variety of factors set the style of a water garden; these include its shape, the selection and placement of its plantings, and the garden around it. A water garden can be designed to blend in with an existing garden style, or it can be used to help establish a style. Fiberglass pools come in a variety of predetermined shapes, but the availability of flexible liners lets you design nearly any shape you like. For more on selecting and installing liners, see chapter 2.

Formal gardens feature geometric shapes and balanced, mirror-image plantings. They are tranquil and elegant to look at. For a formal garden, a rectangle, oval, or round pool is ideal; all are available in fiberglass. For a larger rectangular or L-shaped pool than is commonly available, you can use a flexible liner. Begin by building a frame of pressure-treated wood or cement blocks if the soil is not stable enough to hold the desired shape when you dig. You can also use a flexible liner for an oval or round pool.

Siting is also important to achieving a balanced, formal look: Center a formal pool across the main sight line of the garden—at the end of a prominent path or centered in the yard and surrounded by ground covers or lawn, for example. Edgings such as bricks or flagstones are effective for formal pools. Balanced

A small space calls for a simple, elegant design such as this brick-edged pool rimmed with dwarf mondo grass (Ophiopogon *spp.). A gravel walkway and clipped hedges accent the garden's shape, while pots of annuals at the corners add height and color.*

A riotous mix of tropical and hardy plants fill this informal water garden to capacity. Water lilies and lotus leaves cover much of the water's surface, but a variety of floating-leaved plants add contrasting shapes, colors, and textures. Ferns and striking marginal plants provide a bold leafy backdrop.

Visualizing Your Design

Before you move a shovelful of soil, take time to evaluate your design. Once you've settled on a size and shape, lay a folded tarp on the ground or arrange a hose or rope to outline the general shape of the garden. (Don't lay a dark-colored tarp on the lawn on a sunny day; heat buildup can kill the grass.) Using a tarp or a hose to visualize your design makes it easy to "move" the water garden this way and that or adjust its size and shape until it suits your purpose. Look at the proposed design from all angles. Make sure you are able to see the water from key vantage points — both indoors and out. Also evaluate whether the size and shape are suitable and whether the backdrop you plan needs to be extended or modified. If you are planning a freeform shape, look carefully at the curves and adjust them, if necessary, so they flow smoothly. For economy's sake, use a compact pool and compare the size you choose with available pond liners.

plantings, both in the water garden and around it, complete the formal look. In a rectangular garden this could mean two water lilies flanked by matching groups of marginal plants, perhaps cannas and pickerel rush, for example.

Informal water gardens feature sweeping, natural-looking curves and asymmetrical balance, so nearly any shape works. Fiberglass inserts come in small, simple shapes as well as large, complex ones. Flexible liners allow you to design any shape you like, from a simple crescent to an irregular curvilinear shape. Keep in mind that broadly sweeping curves are generally most effective from a design standpoint and because a liner must be folded to fit the designed shape. Also, a compact shape uses the liner most efficiently. While a narrow garden designed with zigzags wastes liner each time the direction changes, compact shapes (such as a large, irregular oval, for example) waste very little liner.

For a pleasing effect, plantings should still be balanced, but here asymmetry is the rule. Balance a large clump of cannas or cattails, for example, with a grouping of smaller marginal plants and a water lily. For more on selecting plants, see chapter 4.

As you design on an overlay, remember to allow space for edgings such as flagstone around the pond and plantings to blend it into the surrounding landscape. Edging also covers up slight irregularities in the rim of the pond, including places where it is not perfectly level. Keep safety in mind when designing edging: Flagstone and other edgings should extend over the liner by not more than 2 or 3 inches and should be securely cemented in place. Also consider incorporating a fountain or moving water, space for a bog garden or plantings of shallow-water plants, or elements of a wildlife pond in your design. You'll find more information on these features in the pages that follow.

MOVING WATER

It's surprisingly easy to incorporate the sight and sound of splashing water via a fountain, bubbler, waterfall, or spillway. These features add movement and sparkle to your pond, and they also add valuable oxygen to the water to benefit fish. Moving water also creates white noise, which helps screen out unwanted sounds of the world beyond your garden. Fountains and waterfalls require a pump and often are operated in combination with a filter. For more information on these, see "Selecting Pumps, Filters, and Lighting" on page 48.

Fountains. A fountain can be added to any size pond simply by attaching it to a submersible pump. Select a pump suited to the size of your pond. Remember that water lilies prefer still water, so especially in a small pond, select a fountain that produces only a gentle spray or bubbling action. Fountainheads — in brass, stainless steel, and black plastic — are available that attach directly to a pump. Different spray patterns are also available, including a mushroom-shaped spray, a simple upright spray, and a three-tiered formal fountain. A variety of fountains shaped like fish, frogs, and other creatures is also available, piped and ready for a pond. These need to be set on stacks of bricks in the pond or on its edge, and are connected to the pump via tubing. For fountains with easily clogged, tiny-diameter openings, a filter is a good investment to prevent the spray pattern from being distorted. In areas where water freezes, fountains, pumps, and connecting pipes or tubing need to be drained and kept dry over winter.

A wall fountain is easy to install above a small pool in even the tiniest garden. Unless you can hide the tubing in the wall, use copper pipe to bring water from the pool up to the fountainhead. It gradually takes on an attractive patina and becomes nontoxic to goldfish. Another option for a small garden is a fountain or piped statue that sprays water onto a layer of gravel or rocks suspended on several layers of hardware cloth above a reservoir with a pump. A deep plastic tub sunk in the ground works well for a reservoir.

Waterfalls. Creating a waterfall takes considerably more planning than adding a fountain, but is well worth the effort. Sometimes a series of small, connected pools is the perfect solution for a sloping, awkward site.

Fiberglass inserts with spillways are available and make creating a waterfall on a sloping site relatively easy. Simply position the spillway insert above a second pool with the spillway overlapping the lower pool. (The second pool can be another fiberglass pool or one made with a flexible liner.) Use a hose to check the water flow and the position of the two pools before you backfill around them. Also be sure to check that both are level. You can design a series of pools down a sloping site with these inserts. A pump in the lowest pool connected to tubing will return the water to the top of the falls. For best results, run flexible tubing through rigid PVC pipe and bury the return pipe in a shallow trench or cover it with mulch. Flexible tubing alone can be compressed by rocks or by people

Water doesn't have to be the only thing moving in the garden. In this garden, a carefully positioned spillstone creates a tunnel of water for an outdoor train.

This wall fountain and series of pools provide the perfect focal point for a formal garden. The beds filled with irises on either side of the spillway are designed for moisture-loving plants. Water from the lowest level keeps the soil saturated by seeping through a gap in the brick.

A series of waterfalls can be the perfect solution for a sloping site. They can connect several pools or, as in this garden, simply create a dramatic ribbon of water. A single liner underneath the rocks keeps the water from seeping away. Use mortar to hold the rocks in place and direct the water.

standing on it; the PVC pipe also allows you to pull out the tubing for inspection if trouble arises in the line.

When designing a system with a waterfall, make the bottom pond of greater capacity than the top pond. The bottom pond should be large enough so that when the pump starts, the volume of water needed to cause the top pond to overflow, thus starting the waterfall, does not unduly lower the water in the bottom pond or it will look unattractive. Conceal the end of the tube, where it flows into the topmost pool, with rocks or plants to create a natural look. The pump can also send water to a filter outside the pond before returning it to the top pool.

Flexible liners provide other options for creating features with moving water. You can design a series of pools with a single liner under all of them. Covering the liner and creating the falls takes great patience and skill, however. The width of the watercourse needs to narrow where you plan to have it go over the falls. Set a foundation stone or stones in the narrow area and place a flat spillstone on top of it. Test the flow of water with a watering can. The spillstone should slope slightly toward the lower pool and project over the foundation stones, directing the water out rather than down, so it makes a nice sound as it spills into the lower pool. If it dribbles down the face of the foundation stones, reposition the spillstone or select a different one. Once you are pleased with the result, mortar the stones into place on top of the liner as you would to install edging. Also mortar in any stones needed to direct the water over the spillstone. (Use mortar sparingly to maintain a natural look.) See "Edging Options" on page 44 for mixtures and treatments required to neutralize mortar that might come in contact with the water.

SHALLOW WATER AND BOG GARDENS

A water garden is hardly complete without space for plants that thrive in shallow water or the constantly moist conditions of a bog garden. Marginals and floating-leaved plants frame the water garden, soften its edges, shade the water, and add a wealth of color and texture in the process.

Marginal plants, such as cattails (*Typha* spp.), grow in constantly moist soil or in standing water up to a certain depth depending on the species. Floating-

leaved plants grow in shallow water (they are not recommended for constantly moist soil) and as their name suggests, their leaves float on the water's surface, much like water lilies. For information on selecting and growing these plants, see "Marginal and Floating-leaved Plants" on page 95.

Some preformed fiberglass pools come with shallow shelves around the edges to set containers of marginal and floating-leaved plants on. Pools made with flexible liners are often dug with a shallow shelf around their edges for the same reason. These offer a simple way to incorporate marginal and floating-leaved plants, but they can pose problems. For one thing, they restrict pot size and placement in the pond. In addition, hungry raccoons searching for fish and snails are likely to knock plants off the shelves and into deep water. This isn't necessarily fatal for the plants, but it can become annoying.

One option is to use stacks of clean bricks or weathered cinderblocks on the bottom of the pool to place marginals and floating-leaved plants anywhere you choose. (Adjust the height of the stack to position the top of the pot at the proper depth.) That way, you can group plants in any combination you like and not be restricted to the pond edges.

A bog garden that adjoins your pond is a more flexible option that can provide space for a wealth of plants that thrive in moist soil. An adjoining bog garden is easy to design and install with a flexible liner pond. Simply design the main pond shape and then add areas—of any size—for bog plantings. See "Creating Bog Gardens" on page 42 for details on making a bog garden.

WILDLIFE PONDS

A water garden can be the centerpiece of a landscape designed to attract birds, butterflies, and other wildlife. Traditionally, water gardens are constructed with nearly vertical sides, which discourage some types of wildlife from entering the water. Fortunately, with flexible liners it's easy to give wildlife access to water.

Birds and other wildlife need an approach to the water with a gradual grade and a nonslip surface to walk on. Butterflies and beneficial insects will light on rocks that stand partially above the water's surface. One way to provide these conditions is to create a stone beach on one or more sides of the garden. See "Edging Options" on page 44 for details on making a beach. Birds and other

Including a rocky beach with shallow water makes a pond attractive to birds, butterflies, beneficial insects, and a variety of wildlife. Many animals are also attracted to the sound of moving water.

wildlife will use the beach for drinking and bathing. Since birds are wary of water that is more than 2 or 3 inches deep, make the beach area nearly level and cover it with a mix of washed pea gravel and river rock. Arrange the rocks so that a few good-size ones emerge from the water that small birds, butterflies, and beneficial insects can land on. Birds will alight on a branch that emerges from shallow water before entering the water to bathe. They are also attracted by the sound of moving water, so a fountain or waterfall will bring more birds.

Design your pond so that the beach area is in a sunny spot, about 15 feet from trees and shrubs. That way, bathing birds can keep an eye out for predators and will have time to fly for cover. (Birds can't fly quickly with wet feathers.) Mammals such as squirrels, chipmunks, and rabbits can approach the shallow water from the safety of the underbrush. Plants that provide seeds, berries, and nuts—especially native species—are ideal for a wildlife garden.

Moving Water Without the Pond

You can add moving water to a garden without actually having a pond. A Japanese-style feature like this one can be constructed by placing a pump in an underground reservoir such as a large tub. Surround the tub with a liner that catches all the water and returns it to the reservoir. Cover the reservoir with sturdy hardware cloth and then conceal it with gravel.

PLANNING FOR CLEAR WATER

Surprisingly enough, decisions made at the design and installation stage can affect how easy it is to maintain clear, sparkling water in a water garden. Plants and the number of fish also affect water quality. Here are some factors to consider.

Pool Size. In general, the water in larger water gardens tends to stay clearer than it does in smaller ones. Because of the larger volume of water, a large garden maintains a more stable, cooler summer temperature than a small one. The tiny suspended algae that create murky water thrive in warm, sunlit pools. For this reason, if you are planning a pool that will hold less than 100 gallons, consider a site that receives 1 to 2 hours of shade during the hottest part of the day.

Pool Depth. Deep water also helps maintain clear water because it favors cooler, more stable summer temperatures. Avoid installing a water garden that is less than 15 inches deep. (Spillways, where water is constantly moving, can be shallower.) A depth of between 18 and 24 inches is ideal, but water gardens can be deeper. Koi enthusiasts prefer ponds that range from 4 to 5 feet deep. If you live in the coldest zones, make at least part of the pond 3 feet deep to provide extra winter protection for hardy water lilies.

Planting for Clear Water. The plants you select also help ensure clear water. Water lilies and other floating-leaved plants shade the water, thus slightly reducing the temperature and blocking light that algae need to grow. Submerged plants compete directly with algae for nutrients, also controlling their growth. See "Planting, Stocking, and Clear Water" on page 56 for specific planting recommendations.

Pumps and Filters. When attached to a fountain or waterfall, a pump adds movement and sound to a water garden. In the process, it adds oxygen to the water, which fish and other pond residents require. A variety of filters can be used in conjunction with a pump to filter out suspended matter and to break down toxic ammonia fish waste.

CHAPTER 2:
INSTALLING A WATER GARDEN

Depending on the size of your water garden, the installation process, from digging the hole to filling the garden with water, can take as little as a day or a weekend. Large water gardens can take considerably longer. Whatever size garden you are installing, don't rush the process, especially if you plan on digging it by hand. Digging is hard work, especially when you are moving layers of hard-packed subsoil up out of a hole. Before planting a newly filled water garden or stocking it with fish, read "Testing and Treating the Water" on page 55.

At one time, water gardens were constructed primarily of poured concrete, an expensive but long-lasting option. Concrete pools still hold appeal for some gardeners, but they should be installed by an expert, since they can crack and leak if not constructed and poured properly. Today, other long-lasting, easy-to-install options are available, and the vast majority of gardeners take the do-it-yourself route and use preformed pools or flexible liners to create water gardens. Each has advantages. Read the following descriptions to determine which of the two is the best option for you.

This lush water garden abounds with color and texture. Water lilies and duckweed dot the mirrorlike surface, and a mix of marginal plants offer season-long interest because of their contrasting leaf shapes and colors. Pink astilbe and a lavender Japanese iris decorate the shoreline.

Do not use new lining materials designed for swimming pools. Many of these are chemically treated to discourage the growth of algae, and they can harm or kill plants and fish. Preformed pools and liners designed for water gardens are made to be safe for fish and plants. Also, they are black or dark gray rather than swimming-pool blue or aquamarine. That's because a black liner looks more natural, gives the illusion of depth, highlights the reflective surface of the water, and helps the water warm up sooner in spring, encouraging earlier growth. By summer, the sides are covered by beneficial, mosslike algae and the water surface is partially covered with foliage, preventing excess heat buildup. A black liner also contrasts with the colors of the fish and flowers, thus highlighting them.

PREFORMED POOLS

Also called preformed or prefabricated shells, the best preformed pools are made of black or dark gray fiberglass and are thick enough ($1/4$ inch) to hold water when they are above ground, without side support. When properly installed, a good-quality preformed pool lasts 50 years or more and should come with a lengthy guarantee. Avoid models that are made of materials of lower quality than fiberglass, and particularly avoid pools with flexible sides that do not maintain their shape when filled with water without support. Pools with flexible sides are difficult to install because they change shape as you backfill around them, resulting in a top edge that is not level.

Preformed pools come in many shapes and sizes, from rectangular or round to kidney-shaped and freeform. Depth varies from 13 to 18 inches, depending on the model selected. Models with spillway lips, which can be used to create waterfalls, are also available. (A spillway can pour into another preformed pool or into one created with a flexible liner.) Size can run from less than 100 gallons to more than 500. Although preformed pools are more expensive than flexible liners, they are easy to install, tough, and durable.

FLEXIBLE LINERS

Two types of flexible liners are suitable for creating a water garden: PVC and rubber. Both are sold in grades by thickness, measured in mils (one thousandth of an inch). Thicker liners cost more, but they are more durable and last longer. Avoid inexpensive polyethylene liners, which simply don't last long enough to warrant doing the work of installing them.

One advantage of flexible liners is that they allow you to create a water garden in nearly any shape or size. Depth can vary from 15 to 30 inches or more. Generally, flexible liners are available in precut sizes, but some dealers offer rolls in widths up to 50 feet and lengths to 200 feet. You can adapt a flexible liner to fit a site because there are no preset sizes or shapes to deal with. You can also modify a design as you dig — if you uncover a rock outcrop or enormous boulder, for example, or if you simply decide to change the shape of the garden because of a sudden inspiration. (If you suspect this may happen, it's best to order the liner *after* you've finished excavating.)

It's a good idea to protect either type of flexible liner to prevent tears and punctures. A 1- to 2-inch layer of sand works fine on the bottom, but geotextile fabric underlay provides better protection for the sides of the garden. Old carpet also provides serviceable protection. A geotextile underlay protects the waterproof liner by preventing rocks and other sharp objects from working their way through the soil and puncturing it. Some grades of rubber liners, including GeoPond and UltiLiner, come with geotextile bonded to the rubber, eliminating the need for a separate underlayment. Rocks that would puncture a conventional rubber liner merely dent bonded liners.

Flexible liners also provide an option for fixing leaky concrete pools. Simply buy a flexible liner of the appropriate size and lay it over the concrete shell. (Remove any decorative stone or brick coping before putting in the liner.) Be sure to smooth out the concrete first; use a layer of geotextile under the liner if there are sharp edges that may puncture or cut it. Re-edge the garden as you would a flexible liner pond.

PVC Liners. PVC (polyvinyl chloride) comes in several thicknesses, but 32-mil, 2-ply PVC is the best grade for a water garden. Although 16- and 20-mil grades are available, they puncture too easily and are not long-lasting enough for a

satisfactory water garden. Properly installed, the 32-mil PVC liners last for 10 years or more. One drawback is that they deteriorate over the years and become brittle from exposure to the ultraviolet rays of the sun. Cover any exposed edges with stones or other edging materials to protect them from the sun's rays. Also keep your pool filled to the top to reduce exposure.

Rubber Liners. Rubber liners are the longest-lasting flexible liners readily available. They do not degrade in the presence of ultraviolet light and are also more elastic than PVC, making them easier to install. Fish-grade EPDM rubber is the standard available in North America. Avoid EPDM rubber roofing material, which is toxic to fish. Properly installed, a 45-mil liner will last 20 years or more. Rubber liners bonded to geotextile (GeoPond and UltiLiner) are 60 mil thick. These resist tears and punctures as well and are generally sold with a lifetime guarantee.

EXAMINING YOUR SITE

Before you purchase a liner or begin excavating, take a close look at your site to identify any problems you may encounter. Here are some factors to consider.

Check the Slope. Water always finds true level, so it is imperative that the edges of your water garden are level as well. If the edges are perfectly level, the water fills to the same point all the way around the pond. If they are not, the water looks lopsided, high on one side and low on the other. Of course it's the edges that are out of sync, not the water, but it doesn't look that way. In any case, the result is disconcerting.

Few sites are absolutely level to begin with; check the slope before you dig so you know in advance what corrections you'll need to make. See the illustration on page 29 for directions on how to check the slope. Also check throughout the installation process to make sure the garden remains level. If the slope is gradual, you can simply make adjustments as you dig, add sand to the lower side if the difference is less than 2 inches; otherwise use bricks or cinder blocks. Use a felt-tip marker to indicate where the string is on each stake, then remove the strings; they'll just be in the way as you dig. If the slope is steep, see "Slopes," under "Dealing with Problem Sites," on page 32.

Checking the Slope

Pound in a stake at what appears to be the highest point and additional stakes at lower points around the site. Tie a string to the base of the top stake, hang a line level on it, and tie the string to one of the lower stakes. Push the string up the base of the stake until the bubble in the level indicates it is level. The amount of slope you will need to correct for is the distance from the top of the soil to the string.

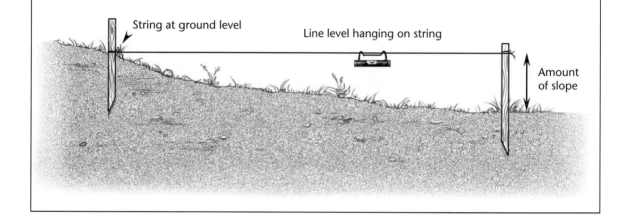

String at ground level

Line level hanging on string

Amount of slope

Look for Problems. Check your base map (see "Selecting the Perfect Site," page 4) or call local suppliers or the utility numbers listed in the front of many phone directories, to verify that your site isn't near any buried electrical cables, gas lines, or cable TV lines. If you suspect your site has a high water table or rock outcrops or boulders lurking under the soil, dig a few test holes to find out. See "Dealing with Problem Sites," page 30, if you encounter any of these problems.

Consider Safety. A water garden presents quite a temptation for both your own small children and those from the neighborhood. Consult local building and zoning authorities to see if a water garden must be fenced in your area. Generally, ponds under 24 inches do not require fencing. If your children are very small, you may want to wait to install a water garden until they are old enough to be taught to maintain a safe distance from it. To add the sight and sound of water without its inherent dangers, consider adding a small wall fountain or a recirculating water feature. See "Moving Water" on page 15 for suggestions.

DEALING WITH PROBLEM SITES

Some sites present challenges, but they are not reason enough to give up on having a water garden. Here are some common situations you might encounter and suggestions for dealing with them.

Runoff. The best time to evaluate runoff is during a rainstorm. Dress for the weather and go outside to figure out which direction(s) the water takes when it runs off your property. Also look to see where water stands after a storm. You may find that adjusting the location of your water garden will move it out of the path of the storm water. Adjusting the slope slightly can sometimes correct a problem as well. Another option is to raise the height of the pond by building a semiraised pool.

Water also can be redirected by building earth berms or digging swales. Decide where the water needs to be redirected and use a series of stakes to mark off where a berm or swale would need to be located to redirect it. A swale needs to be deep enough to accommodate runoff during the height of a storm and needs to have an even bottom so water doesn't collect along its length. A berm should be twice as wide as it is high — a 1-foot-tall berm should be about 2 feet wide at its top, for example. When you dig the water garden, use the subsoil (the clayey soil under the topsoil) to build the base of the berm, then cover it with topsoil. Plant the berm or swale with lawn grass or with low shrubs and tough perennials.

That said, locating a water garden in a spot that receives runoff doesn't always pose insurmountable problems. If you maintain a strictly organic landscape — avoiding the use of all chemical fertilizers, pesticides, fungicides, and herbicides — and if storm water does not run over the yard of a neighbor who does use these products, then runoff may not pose a problem if it gets in your pond. However, runoff adds silt and can cause severe structural damage if it goes under your pond, possibly lifting up its bottom. You will have to clean out the debris that flows into the water garden periodically, and it will sometimes overflow its banks. Organic fertilizer materials such as composted manure cause algal blooms, and thus green water, if they wash into the water, but won't cause long-term problems. Be aware that some organic pesticides, including rotenone and ryania, are highly toxic to fish.

Avoid siting a water garden in an area with a high water table, which will push a liner up out of the ground. This formal round garden is located near a natural pond but is well uphill, out of the way of rising ground water.

High Water Table. Springs in your area, damp spots that appear mysteriously in spring, and a seasonally wet basement are all signs that ground water or a high water table may be a problem on a selected site. Ground water that rises to the surface under a pond pushes upward on a liner or preformed pool. The water releases oxygen that causes a flexible liner to balloon up. Ground water can force a preformed pool out of the ground entirely.

The easiest way to cope with ground water is to install the pool so its bottom is well above the highest point the water table reaches. Installing a shallower pool may solve the problem, but you can also create a raised or semiraised pool so the bottom is above the water table. See "Rock Outcrops and Other Conditions" on page 32 for information on building a raised pool.

Another solution is to dig a trench along the bottom of the site to drain off excess ground water. Place perforated pipe in the trench, cover it with coarse gravel, and top it with a layer of landscape fabric before installing the water garden. The trench must lead downhill so it drains properly. Consider directing it into a low area that you can plant with perennials that appreciate damp soil, such as ferns, astilbes, Siberian iris, and other marginals.

If your site features springs that flow year-round, you may be able to install a clay-lined pond that is kept filled by the natural water flow. In order to accommodate a typical water garden, however, the water must warm to over 70°F. A high water table or springs that flow seasonally are not in themselves enough to keep a clay-lined lily pond filled satisfactorily, however. Consult your local water management authority for advice and recommendations on local experts who can advise you.

Slopes. A series of small, interconnected water gardens is a delightful solution for a sloping site. See "Waterfalls" on page 16 for more information. Another option is to install one large water garden as shown below. Be sure to redirect water flow from above the site around the edges of the garden using earth berms or swales.

Rock Outcrops and Other Conditions. If you suspect that rock outcrops, large boulders, or other obstacles lie under a potential site, you can look for an entirely different site that will be easier to dig. Another option, which takes more work but can lead to spectacular results, is to let the rocks help determine the shape of the pool. In this case, you should wait until after you've dug the garden to order a flexible liner. Start by digging some test holes to determine where the rocks lie, and then dig out the hole for the water garden (or a series of holes for connected gardens). Fine-tune the design for the garden as you dig. You may uncover an outcrop or boulder that would be spectacular with a pond nestled at its base, for example. Dig the soil off rocks you want to expose and let the rain wash them.

You may also choose to build a raised pool, and for this, a rigid fiberglass liner is ideal. Remove soil as deep as you can, then level the site and add 1 to 2 inches of sand to create a level base for the garden. Then backfill around the liner with a wide berm of soil that can be planted with perennials, ground covers, or

Sloping Site Installations

To install a water garden on a sloping site, use one of the methods shown here. Method 1, which is the best way, requires more soil removal. Dig into the slope and use a wall behind it to create a level site. This method can be used with either a preformed pool or a flexible liner. Method 2 uses an earth berm on the lower side and a swale above the pond to redirect runoff. In this case, a preformed pool is easiest to install because it would support the weight of the water and a retaining wall or berm would provide supplemental support and insulation. A flexible-liner pond could not be supported by a mounded berm of soil; a rigid frame, constructed of cinderblocks or landscape timbers, would be required on the lower side.

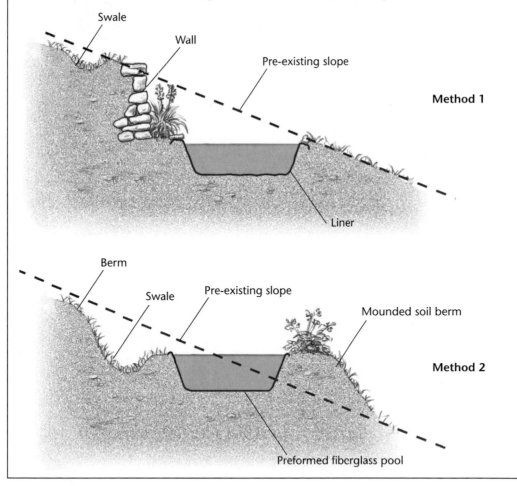

Swale

Wall

Pre-existing slope

Method 1

Liner

Berm

Swale

Pre-existing slope

Mounded soil berm

Method 2

Preformed fiberglass pool

There's no doubt that a rocky site presents challenges for installing a water garden, but it can also provide a huge payoff. This stream, underlaid with a flexible liner, illustrates some of the effects you can create on a difficult site. Dwarf conifers, azaleas, and a variety of rock garden plants create a convincing mountainscape.

low shrubs. It's also possible to create a raised or semiraised pool with a brick or stone wall around it. Consult an expert for construction advice. Be aware that raised and semiraised pools, especially those not surrounded by a wide berm of earth, will freeze deeper and more often in winter than otherwise identical in-ground ponds. An earth berm also helps moderate water temperatures in summer. See "Fall and Winter Care" on page 69 for information on dealing with winter conditions.

Not Enough Sun. Although a site that receives 6 or more hours of sun per day is ideal, there are ways to enjoy a water garden on a lightly shaded site. See chapter 4 for recommendations on water lilies, marginals, and floating-leaved plants

With flexible liners, the size and shape of the hole you dig determine the size, shape, and contours of your pond. This makes it easy to adapt the garden to site conditions such as rocky terrain. This freeform water garden features a waterfall tumbling over a rough stone wall and plenty of space for shallow-water marginals.

that grow in light shade. Hostas, astilbes, and ferns also make fine plants for damp, shady conditions.

Selective pruning may increase the amount of sun a site receives. Thin out low-hanging branches or remove trees or shrubs to let in the light. Hire an arborist to do the work for you if you would need to climb a ladder to accomplish the pruning required.

Fall leaves are a major headache in water gardens located in shady sites. The leaves settle at the bottom of the pond and decompose over winter, releasing gases that can kill fish if they build up sufficiently under the ice. Stretch plastic netting or screens over the garden in fall and lift them off every few days to remove the leaves. See "Removing Leaves" on page 71 for other options.

INSTALLATION BASICS

Whether you are installing a preformed pool or a flexible liner, start by removing existing vegetation from the site, including a shallow 12- to 15-inch strip around the garden to allow space for edging. With a sharp spade, cut around strips of lawn grass, slice under them, and then roll them up. Place them upside down on the compost pile to discard them or use them to repair damaged spots in the lawn. If you plan on replanting the grass up to the edge of a flexible liner pond, set it in a shady spot and keep it moist.

> ### TIPS FOR SUCCESS
>
> #### DIG SMART
>
> Always dig with a straight back and bent knees, and don't overload the spade or shovel. When lifting a shovelful of soil out of the hole, lift with your knees, not your back. Never twist and throw soil; instead turn your feet and body first, then toss the soil onto a tarp or into a wheelbarrow. You may find it's easier to loosen the soil in the bottom of the hole with a garden fork or a mattock, then scoop it up with a shovel. Above all, take frequent breaks and drink plenty of water. Stop *before* you are tired. You are much more likely to injure yourself if you continue digging after you are exhausted.

Mark the location of the pool following the directions for the type of liner you are installing (see below). Then begin to dig. If you are concerned about the effort required to dig the garden yourself, hire someone to dig the hole and help you install the liner. (Bribing friends with a fabulous dinner may or may not work for digging, but could suffice for liner installation!) After that, the work required is minimal. If you are installing a large water garden and there is room to maneuver around the site, consider hiring someone with the appropriate equipment to dig it for you. Or rent the equipment and dig it yourself; a mid-size garden tractor with a backhoe is perfect for the job.

If you are dealing with a sloping site, do not add soil at the bottom of a hole to try to level the foundation. Even after it is tamped in place, the weight of the water will compress the soil over time at unequal rates. This will make the top edge of the pond uneven. Instead, dig down and create a level foundation in the subsoil.

Throughout the process, try to preserve your garden's topsoil and keep it separate from the clay subsoil underneath. Skim the topsoil off the site first and set it aside on a tarp or pile it up in a convenient location. Place the subsoil on a tarp or in a wheelbarrow or garden cart. It is useful for filling in around edging or along a preformed pool. It can also be used to build earth berms to redirect runoff, fill potholes in the lawn, or create a base layer in a raised bed. However you use it, be sure to top it with a thick layer of topsoil if you plan to grow plants on the site.

INSTALLING PREFORMED POOLS

To mark the site for a preformed pool, place the pool in the desired location, right-side up. Pound stakes into the ground around its edges. Many preformed pools have shallow marginal shelves on one or more edges; mark these with stakes as well, then remove the pool and begin digging. Most preformed pools have sloping sides, but if you have sandy or crumbly soil, you'll have to exaggerate the slope as you dig so the soil doesn't crumble down and fill the hole as you empty it. You can slice directly down through clay soil to closely outline the shape of the pool.

Check the depth of the hole periodically; ultimately, the excavation should be 1 to 2 inches deeper than the preformed pool to accommodate a layer of sand in the bottom to level the pool. Measuring the hole carefully (width and depth) helps you judge whether the size and shape are correct, but you will probably need to place the pool in the hole several times to get the size exactly right. Preformed pools are more cumbersome than heavy, but plan on having one or more helpers on hand for this process. When the hole is the correct size, take the pool out one last time.

Use a carpenter's level to check the bottom to see that it is relatively level, adjust it if necessary, then line the bottom with 1 to 2 inches of sand to level it accurately. Check the edges of the pool to make sure they are level, too. Scrape soil off high spots and add soil or sand (firmly tamped in place) to raise low spots. Use bricks, stones, or cinderblocks, firmly packed with sand or subsoil, to raise spots that are more than 2 inches too low. Avoid lowering the rim of the pond below the grade of the surrounding site.

Lower the preformed pool into place. Press it firmly into the sand, then use a straight 2x4 and a carpenter's level to make sure the pool is absolutely level — check end to end and across it at several points. Remove the pool and rake the sand, or add and remove sand as necessary, until it is level to within $1/4$ inch.

Begin slowly filling the pond with water. As it fills, pack subsoil (sand is better) around the outside of the fiberglass pool. This keeps the pressure on the walls the same inside and out. If you pack too much soil on the outside, you can press the wall in, resulting in an uneven top edge. Check periodically throughout the process to make sure the pool remains level. Once it is full, install the edging of your choice to cover up the fiberglass edge of the pool. See "Edging Options" on page 44 for ideas as well as directions for draining and cleaning out the pool before adding plants or fish.

INSTALLING FLEXIBLE LINERS

Since the shape, size, depth, and structural integrity of a flexible-liner garden depend on the hole you dig, PVC and rubber liners offer a variety of installation options. Most gardeners start the process by calculating how large a liner they need to create the garden they have designed. It's easy to vary a design as you dig, however. While adding a beach to provide wildlife access won't greatly change the overall liner size required, wait until after you have finished excavating to purchase a liner if you suspect you'll want to make major changes, such as making the garden larger or smaller, changing its shape to avoid rock outcrops, or adding a large area for a bog garden.

Calculating Liner Size. Determining liner size is simple, even with freeform shapes. First determine the maximum width and length of the garden. (It helps to determine the smallest square or rectangle the garden would fit in.) Then determine the maximum depth (marginal shelves do not affect the overall liner size required). See "Planting, Stocking, and Clear Water" on page 56 for guidelines on determining depth. To determine the liner width required, add twice the depth plus 2 feet for edging. (Experienced installers may only add one foot for edging, 6 inches for each side.) Do the same for the length. For example, a 2-foot-deep pool that is 6 feet wide and 8 feet long needs a liner that is 12 feet wide and 14 feet long.

Digging and Installation. To mark out the garden, dig, and install it, use the step-by-step sequence of photos that follow. Throughout the process, check the edges of the hole frequently with a carpenter's level set on top of a *straight* 2 x 4 to make sure the edges remain level. If your pond is large, place 1 to 3 stakes in the center of the pond and level them with the correct height of the rim of the pond. Then use the level stakes to check and adjust the edges.

In most cases, dig the sides at a 75-degree angle. Slope the sides closer to a 45-degree angle if your soil is sandy or crumbly, although this reduces level space for planting containers on the bottom of the pool. You can dig marginal shelves or create a separate bog garden for marginals and floating-leaved plants. See "Creating Bog Gardens" on page 42 for details. See "Edging Options" on page 44 for information on creating a beach for wildlife or edging the garden with stones, flagstones, or plants.

Step 1. Outline the water garden with a hose, rope, or sprinkling of sand. Use stakes and string, along with a carpenter's square, to establish the shape of square or rectangular gardens. Use a central stake and a length of string to mark the edges of a round garden. Strip off any grass or other vegetation.

After outlining your water garden, step back and make sure the shape is pleasing and that you can see it from key vantage points. Adjust the shape before you dig.

Step 2. Dig the pool to the desired depth and shape. The pond shown on pages 39 to 42 has earthen shelves for marginal and floating-leaved plants. Shelves should be 9 to 12 inches wide and 9 to 12 inches below the top edge of the excavation. Also remove sod around the edges to prepare the site for an edging of rocks or flagstones.

Sand provides excellent protection for the floor of the pond, but it works its way to the bottom of the excavation over time. Use geotextile to protect the sides.

Step 3. When the garden is deep enough, dig an 18-inch-wide area on one side so that it is 1 to 2 inches deeper than the rest. When you clean out the pool, fish and other residents will gather at this end, making them easy to scoop up. Also set the pump or siphon at this point during clean-out to remove all the water. Check again with a 2x4 and carpenter's level to make sure the edges remain level. Scrape soil off high spots and add soil or sand (firmly tamped in place) to raise low spots. Use bricks, stones, or cinderblocks, firmly packed with sand or sub-soil, to raise spots that are more than 2 inches too low. Remove sharp rocks and other objects from the sides and bottom, then line the bottom with 1/2 to 1 inch of builder's sand.

Step 4. Line the sides of the pool with geotextile underlayment or old carpeting to cushion the liner. Skip this step if you are installing a geotextile liner bonded to rubber. If you plan on setting any large rocks on top of the liner, add an extra cushion of old carpeting under the liner to protect it.

After spreading the liner, make sure there is enough "play" to allow it to settle all along the edges of the bottom and the marginal shelves. Also, smooth out wrinkles.

Step 5. Unfold the liner and spread it in the sun to make it more flexible and easier to work with. (You will need at least one helper to handle the liner.) Since heat builds up quickly underneath a liner on a sunny day, don't spread it on the lawn; the heat kills the grass very quickly. Spread the liner in the hole. Liners for large ponds may be extremely heavy: Place them in the excavation while still folded, then unfold. Smooth out the wrinkles and fold or pleat the liner as necessary to fit curves and angles. If it is windy, weigh down the corners of the liner with smooth stones or bricks. Check to be sure edges are level one last time. Adjust them if necessary.

Step 6. Don't begin to fill the garden until the liner is positioned satisfactorily — once it is weighed down by water, you won't be able to adjust the position or add or change folds. When the liner is arranged, fill it with water to within 1 inch of the rim. Then cut off the excess liner, leaving a 6- to 12-inch flap around the edges. Drive 4- to 6-inch spikes or nails into the ground around the edges of the liner to hold the flap in place.

Edging adds a finishing touch to a water garden, but it also plays another important role: It hides and protects the liner.

Step 7. Install the edging around the garden. If you mortar the edging into place, you'll need to drain the pool and clean off the mortar, as described in "Edging Options." Otherwise the mortar releases lime into the pond, which can be damaging to fish and plants.

Step 8. Before adding plants, treat the water for chlorine, chloramide, and ammonia. See "Testing and Treating the Water" on page 55 for details. Wait one to two weeks after treating the water before adding fish, snails, or other creatures.

CREATING BOG GARDENS

Creating a moist-soil garden, or bog garden, along the edge of your water garden is as easy as digging the water garden itself. (True bog gardens provide very acidic conditions for plants—they are usually filled with a mix of half peat and half sand.) Since the bog garden is filled with soil, it needs to be separated from the water garden itself. This can be done by stacking rocks or even upside-down pieces of sod between the two so water slowly seeps into the bog and the soil

Independent Bog Garden

A soil berm *under* the liner separates this bog garden from the adjacent water garden.
A rock hides the liner, which would otherwise be exposed, to create a natural effect.
An independent bog garden must be watered separately.

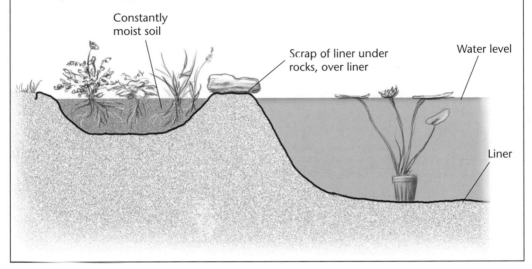

Constantly
moist soil

Scrap of liner under
rocks, over liner

Water level

Liner

Integrated Bog Garden

This design allows water to seep slowly though the permeable layer between the adjoining pool
and bog gardens. Water the bog in dry weather so it does not wick too much water out of the
pool. Otherwise, keeping the pool filled will keep the bog moist.

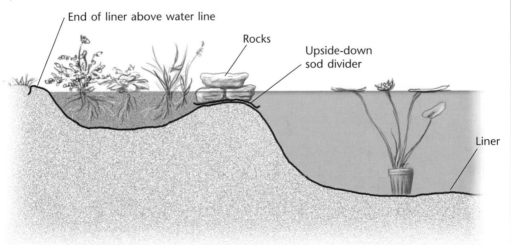

End of liner above water line

Rocks

Upside-down
sod divider

Liner

stays out of the water. Another option is to create an entirely separate bog by leaving an earth barrier *under* the liner. See the illustrations on page 43 for details.

To make a bog garden, simply dig an area any size you like that is about 12 inches deep and extend the water garden liner under the entire area. Punch a few very small holes at intervals in the bottom of the bog garden portion of the liner. (This prevents aerobic conditions in the soil.) Then fill the bog with soil. You can also fill it partially to leave some standing water. Bog gardens also can be free-standing—you don't necessarily even need a water garden to enjoy one. Keep marginals and floating-leaved plants that spread rapidly in containers.

EDGING OPTIONS

You can use a single edging for your water garden, such as brick or flagstone, or for a casual look, use a mix of edgings, including plants, rocks, a beach, and flag-stones. Plan on providing at least some areas with smooth edgings such as brick, flagstone, or even lawn grass, so visitors can walk close to the water. A narrow rim of low ground covers keeps adult visitors off edging not designed to handle foot traffic, but you may have to warn children to stay off the stones or other edging that rims a pond.

Edging, or coping, made of flagstone, pavers, or flat fieldstones should extend over the edge of the water 1 or 2 inches. This conceals the liner, giving the water garden a more attractive edge, and protects it from ultraviolet rays of the sun. Coping can be raised 1 to 2 inches above the surrounding soil surface or it can be set flush with the earth. See the illustrations on pages 46 and 47 for different edging options.

To mortar stone edging in place to provide a secure edge, spread the mortar on galvanized metal lathe (available at hardware stores) and position the stones on top. A 2- to 3-inch mortar base, reinforced with additional layers of metal lathe, is best in areas with freezing winter temperatures. (You may need to shave off a ledge around the edge to accommodate this.) Try to position the stones evenly around the edges, and use mortar sparingly between stones. If your coping will be walked on, it is best to pour a 12- to 18-inch-deep concrete footer to lay it on before the garden is installed.

While a uniform edge, such as all brick or all cut stone, is typical of formal water gardens, a mix of edgings can be effective for an informal pond. This garden primarily features fieldstone edging, but a variety of plants cascades over the edges to create a soft, natural effect.

Beach Design

To create a beach for wildlife, dig a shallow, gentle slope. Then mortar a row of large, rounded rocks onto the edge of the slope as you would to install edging. These keep the washed pea gravel and rounded river rocks that make up the beach from falling to the bottom of the pool. The water should be 2 to 3 inches deep, with many rocks sticking up above the surface to provide perches.

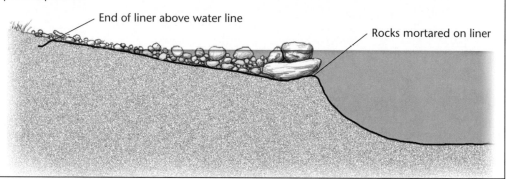

End of liner above water line

Rocks mortared on liner

Formal or Informal Edging

To conceal the liner and create an elegant flagstone or bluestone coping, dig a small shelf at the top of the garden excavation, high and wide enough to accommodate a stack of three decorative bricks. Run the liner behind the bricks and set the coping stones on top of them. Then the garden can be filled to just below the coping, thus also creating a decorative edge.

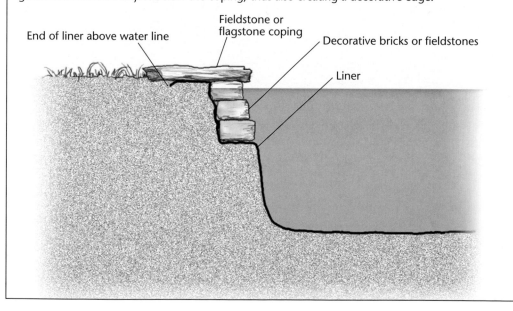

End of liner above water line

Fieldstone or flagstone coping

Decorative bricks or fieldstones

Liner

Angled Rock Edge

For a small garden, consider an angled rock edging to reduce the amount of visible stone around the garden and maximize the water's surface. Dig an angled shelf near the top of the hole, lay down the liner, then fit stones along it as shown. Stones can be mortared in place, if necessary.

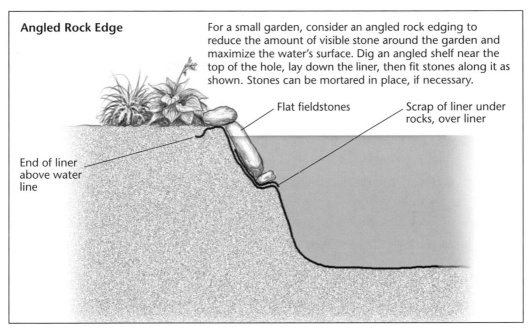

Flat fieldstones

Scrap of liner under rocks, over liner

End of liner above water line

Secure Stone Edging

For the most secure edging, pour a concrete footer along the edge of the pond before digging the site. Run the liner over the footing and mortar edging stones in place. Cement blocks set on firmly packed soil, as shown here, will also provide a firm edging. Large flagstones or fieldstones may be secure without mortar.

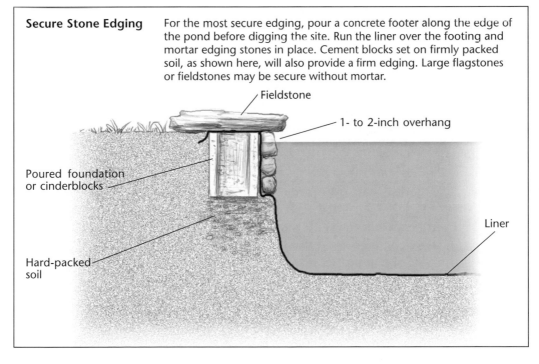

Fieldstone

1- to 2-inch overhang

Poured foundation or cinderblocks

Liner

Hard-packed soil

For mortar, start with premixed mortar or mix one part Portland cement and two parts sand by volume. Then mix with enough water to give the mortar an icinglike consistency. When you have finished mortaring stones in place, let them dry for 24 hours, then drain the pond, remove excess mortar with a stiff brush, and clean any excess out of the pool. Wash any mortar that will be in contact with the water with a mixture of one part vinegar to five parts water or a neutralizing product such as Drylock Etch. Rinse thoroughly and then refill the pool.

Plants as Edgers. Dwarf and low-growing conifers, spreading broad-leaved evergreens, small ornamental grasses, evergreen ground covers, and a variety of other plants make quite satisfactory edgings for water gardens that are both easy to install and inexpensive. When you choose edging plants, keep in mind that they will be growing in normal soil conditions, since water won't leak through the liner. Space them back from the edge so they can overhang it without covering too much of the water surface. Trim them back as necessary. You can also grow grass up to the edge of a water garden, but you will need to hand-trim the edge and remove clippings from the water.

SELECTING PUMPS, FILTERS, AND LIGHTING

Sooner or later, most gardeners decide they want a pump to operate a fountain or filter or lights so they can enjoy their garden in the evening. Running electricity to a water garden can be accomplished any time, but it is easiest during the construction stage, when the site is torn up anyway. To operate any electrical equipment near a water garden, use an outdoor outlet, set back at least 6 feet from the water, that is equipped with a ground fault interrupter (GFI) for greatest safety. These devices cut off power to your pump or other appliance the moment water is detected in contact with the wiring. Have an electrician add a GFI to an existing outlet or have a new circuit with a buried outdoor cable, also equipped with a GFI, installed. The cable should be protected in a conduit so you won't dig into it accidentally. You may be able to save money on the installation charges if you dig the trench for the cable yourself. Extension cords with an integrated GFI are also available and are useful for runs of up to about 100 feet to a pond. Hide them under stones or mulch for aesthetic considerations.

Pumps are the mechanics that move water in a pond. A piped statue like this one can be powered by a fairly small submersible pump—a rating of about 300 gallons per hour is sufficient.

Pump Selection. Pumps come in a confusing array of models and sizes. Submersible pumps, which are placed right in the water, are the most common. Reputable water garden suppliers have charts and other information available that can help you select the best model and connecting equipment for your purposes. Don't buy from a dealer that recommends a one-size-fits-all pump.

Pumps are rated according to the number of gallons per hour (GPH) they can lift the water one vertical foot higher than the pump. The slower they are, the fewer gallons per hour they lift. As the vertical height increases, the number of gallons pumped decreases. For example, a pump that lifts 300 GPH at a height of 1 foot, lifts 270 GPH at 3 feet, 240 GPH at 5 feet, and 130 GPH at 10 feet. If you want to lift 240 GPH 5 feet up to create a waterfall, the above pump is the right size for you. If you want a 240 GPH waterfall 10 feet high, you'll need a larger pump. Pumping water horizontally also puts additional strain on the pump. Each 10 feet of horizontal flow is equivalent to 1 foot of vertical lift.

A lily bubbler, which uses a low lift of water and has a wide, nonrestrictive outlet, won't affect a pump substantially. If you have a waterfall or want a certain fountain spray pattern with either a high lift of water and/or tiny, restrictive outlets, you need to take that into consideration. To select a pump that lifts the water from a lower pool up to a spillway pool or waterfall above it, for example, you need to know how many feet the water needs to be raised vertically up the slope and how many feet the water must be pushed horizontally. When planning a waterfall, keep in mind that every 100 gallons pumped per hour produces a $\frac{1}{2}$-inch-deep flow of water that is 1 inch wide, or a $\frac{1}{4}$-inch-deep flow 2 inches wide. If the spillway you are using is 4 inches wide, you'll only have a trickle. Size the pump according to the flow rate desired. A 200 GPH flow rate will double the depth at the same width.

Calculating Water Volume

To determine how many gallons of water are in your pond, first determine how many cubic feet it contains using the formulas below.

Rectangle. Length in feet × width in feet × depth in feet = cubic feet.

Circle. 3.14 ($\frac{1}{2}$ diameter in feet × $\frac{1}{2}$ diameter in feet) × depth in feet = cubic feet.

Freeform shapes. Break the pond down into a series of rectangles and circles and figure the volumes of each area separately, then add the volumes together.

Each cubic foot contains 7.5 gallons of water, so multiply the total number of cubic feet times 7.5 to determine the total number of gallons.

To select a pump, you also need to know how many gallons there are in your pond and what type of filtration, if any, you are going to use. (Water can go from a filter to the waterfall.) For the volume of preformed pools, refer to the specifications that come with the pool; use the formulas in "Calculating Water Volume" for flexible-liner pools. For mechanical filtration, select a pump that will recirculate the volume of water at least once every two hours. Therefore, assuming a lift of 1 foot, the pump for a 1,000-gallon pond with mechanical filtration should recirculate at least 500 gallons per hour minimum; more gallons per hour is fine. For biological filtration, the water should be recirculated once every 4 to 6 hours. Don't run water too fast through a biological filter, otherwise the bacteria won't have time to do their work.

Filters. Filters remove suspended matter from the water and harbor beneficial bacteria that break down toxic ammonia into nontoxic nitrate. It's possible to have clear water without filtration if you carefully balance the number of fish with the number of submerged plants, water lilies, and other floating-leaved plants. Filtration becomes necessary for a variety of reasons, including an overpopulation of fish, to remove excess suspended silt, and when warm water encourages the growth of algae. There are filters to fit every size pool and price range. Keep in mind that with any kind of filtration—as well as with UV sterilizers, discussed below—submerged plants are still needed to absorb the nitrates resulting from the breakdown of organic matter, including fish waste.

Mechanical filters are available that can be attached to the pump and dropped directly in the water. These clean the water by pushing or pulling it through a series of mats or filters, which need to be cleaned every one to two days during the summer. There are also mechanical filters that can be set outside the pond. Water is pumped out of the pool and into the filter, which needs to be cleaned every two to seven days.

Biological filters, which are typically set up outside the pool, use bacteria grown on filter mats or gravel in a tank or other large container outside the pool to neutralize ammonia and clean the water. (The bacteria are naturally occurring, but most gardeners buy a supply to get the filter up and running quickly.) There are many variations of biological filters. The best types pump the water to an aeration tower. Water then falls down to the bottom of the container and works its

way up through filters and/or layers of gravel filled with beneficial bacteria. Muck is left at the bottom, where it can be flushed out by opening a valve, and clear water flows out the top and back into the garden. Once or twice a month, as needed, gently back-flush the filter using a garden hose.

Biological filters are large, but they can be hidden behind shrubs, fencing, or a shed, and the water can be run back to the pool via tubing or a waterfall. (The top of the filter must be higher than the surface of the pool or waterfall.) Although more expensive than mechanical filters, one advantage of biological filters is that they need cleaning out less often — once or twice a month, depending on the amount of suspended matter trapped in the filter, which is partially dependent on the stocking level of your pool. Because the bacteria must have time to convert the ammonia to nitrite and then to nitrate, water must be circulated more slowly through a biological filter than a mechanical one (once every 4 to 6 hours).

UV Sterilizers. These use ultraviolet light to kill algae and fish pathogens that are free-floating in the water. Koi lovers, who always want clear, healthy pond water, routinely combine a UV sterilizer with biological filtration. Manufacturers give maximum flow rates that should not be exceeded; if water passes through these devices too quickly, the algae and parasites may not be exposed to enough ultraviolet light to kill them. To use a UV sterilizer, select a size that is compatible with recirculating the pond volume once every 4 to 6 hours and use the same pump to power water though the sterilizer on the way to the biological filter. When used properly, they kill algae, eliminating green water. Use a pond vacuum to remove algae that settle on the pond floor.

Lighting. Low-voltage lights designed especially for gardens are easy to install around a water garden. Lighting makes a water garden safer after dark if it is installed in a well-traveled area, such as along the edge of a terrace. It also can be used to create an alluring sitting area after dark. There are also lights designed to be submerged in the water, which can add a magical touch. In addition to the lights, you need a transformer to step down the voltage for the low-voltage systems.

Determining the correct size pump required to power a waterfall like this one can be tricky, but it can also yield spectacular results. You need to take into account how many feet the pump must push water through tubing both vertically and horizontally, as well as how many gallons need to come over the falls per hour to create the desired effect.

CHAPTER 3:

PLANTS, FISH, AND YEAR-ROUND CARE

A brand-new, full-to-the-brim water garden is nearly ready for plants and fish, but not quite. Fortunately, the hard work of digging the garden is behind you. Testing and treating the water to make sure it is safe for fish is a simple matter. And while selecting the right mix of plants to help ensure clear water and a healthy pond takes planning, it's fun to contemplate all the options available. Finally, adding fish and other inhabitants couldn't be easier in a properly planned and planted water garden. In this chapter you'll learn everything you need to know to plant and stock a water garden, as well as how to care for it throughout the year.

TESTING AND TREATING THE WATER

Water from most municipal systems must be treated before it is safe for fish because it may contain chlorine, chlorine dioxide, chloramine, or other additives. (Plants tolerate these additives in the quantities used to treat drinking water, but

Submerged plants, visible just below the water's surface between the pads of this tropical water lily, play a vital role in controlling algae and keeping the water clear. Thin them as necessary (if the fish don't) to keep them from clogging the water.

fish do not.) Although chlorine in water dissipates within a few days, chloramine does not. Call your local water department to determine what additives your water contains.

A variety of water treatment products that neutralize these additives is available. Read the label carefully to determine both what they treat and the proper dosage required. You need to know the total water volume of your garden in order to treat the water; see "Calculating Water Volume" on page 50 for directions. Pond treatments are available that neutralize both chlorine and chlorine dioxide, and remove heavy metals from the water. They also contain a colloid coating that reduces stress for fish by coating their gills and membranes. If your water contains chloramine, use a treatment to neutralize it along with one that neutralizes chlorine and chlorine dioxide.

Although pH is not a problem in most water gardens, it's a good idea to test it before you add fish or other creatures and periodically thereafter. The ideal pH to maintain fish should be close to neutral, 7.0, but water that is slightly acid to slightly alkaline, from 6.8 to 7.4, is very good. (Many plants thrive in more acid conditions, from pH 5.5 to 6.5.) Test kits are available at pet stores and water garden suppliers. Test the pH in the morning three days in a row in a new garden and monthly thereafter if the water is near the limits of the acceptable range. Also test pH if fish appear sluggish but do not show any signs of disease. Commercial products are available to adjust pH. Baking soda, added at one teaspoon per day per 100 gallons, neutralizes water that is too acid as well. If the pH needs adjustment, do it gradually, never more than .5 points per day; too sudden a change stresses the fish.

PLANTING, STOCKING, AND CLEAR WATER

Maintaining clear water and healthy conditions for fish is easy if you select the right mix of plants. Introducing scavengers helps keep the garden clean and healthy as well. It's also important to avoid overstocking the garden with fish. See "Fish for a Water Garden" on page 62 for stocking and care recommendations that help maintain clear water.

Plant your garden anytime after treating the water according to the guidelines below. Then prepare yourself to watch the water turn green. The green

Planting a water garden with the right mix of plants goes a long way toward ensuring clear water and healthy conditions for fish. Plants that shade the water, including water lilies, help control algae, which turn the water green.

Frogs will find their way to water gardens from nearby wetland areas.

water, caused by exploding populations of free-floating, single-celled algae, is the first step in a natural process that establishes a healthy, balanced ecosystem. The water clears naturally within 4 to 6 weeks as the plants become established. Draining the pool and refilling it at this point is the worst thing you can do and only delays the process. Wait a week or two after planting to add fish, snails, and other inhabitants. They won't be harmed by the green water, but they shouldn't be introduced until after the water has cured. This waiting period allows populations of beneficial bacteria to build up before the fish are introduced.

If you can't stand the sight of the green water even for a few weeks, black dye that is safe for fish and plants is available from water garden suppliers. It hides the green color and makes the water look velvety and deep. Adding black dye also highlights plants and fish, hides containers, makes the water very reflective, and reduces the amount of sunlight available to algae. For these reasons, many public gardens use it routinely. To kill algae, use a UV sterilizer.

Proper Planting Proportions. Submerged plants and floating-leaved plants such as water lilies work together to control the free-floating algae that cause green water. For water gardens with under 100 square feet of surface area, plant either 50 bunches or 1 bunch (6 stems) of submerged plants *per square foot* of surface area, whichever is *less*. For gardens with over 100 square feet of surface area, plant one bunch for every 2 square feet.

Select water lilies and other floating-leaved plants that will cover between 60 and 70 percent of the water's surface. In a small garden, it's best to cover more; less coverage will work fine in a large garden because of the greater water volume. See chapter 4 for estimated spreads for water lilies and more information on plant selection.

Scavengers for Natural Cleanup. Snails are the primary scavengers you want to add, but tadpoles play a scavenging role in a pool's ecosystem, too. Stock scavengers at the same rate used for submerged plants. Spring and fall are the best times to add snails, tadpoles, and frogs, which thrive in a pool year-round as long as it does not freeze solid. They bury themselves in the mud at the bottom of the pond to overwinter.

Black Japanese snails *(Viviparus malleatus)* are the best choice for a water garden. These hardworking creatures give birth to live young once or twice a year and eat algae on the sides of the liner and pots as well as along plant stems without consuming the plants themselves. Other species of snails may eat the plants and become overpopulated.

Tadpoles eat leftover fish food and plant debris, while frogs eat insects both in the pond (including mosquito larvae) and outside it. Frogs also eat small fish and tadpoles. If there are wetland areas near your yard, frogs and their tadpoles will probably find their way to your water garden on their own.

PLANTING YOUR WATER GARDEN

Water lilies and other water garden plants may look exotic, but they are surprisingly undemanding and easy to grow. Once your garden is filled with water, plant your choices as recommended below.

Water lilies and most marginal and floating-leaved plants can be planted anytime from spring to early fall. In spring, plant hardy water lilies when water temperatures exceed 55° to 60°F; wait until minimum water temperatures reach 70°F to plant tropicals. Lotuses can only be planted in spring. When potting water lilies and other plants, select a shady location. Lily pads dry out and die quickly when their undersides are exposed to air. Keep them in their moist packing material during the brief period awaiting potting. If the packing material has dried out, moisten it and reseal the packages. Handle plants carefully to avoid damaging them.

Selecting Containers. Plant water lilies, lotuses, marginals, and floating-leaved plants in plastic pans or tubs sold by water garden suppliers, or use ordinary dishpans in dark colors. Pots such as black plastic nursery pots that have been well scrubbed and rinsed are useful as well. Block the drainage holes with stones or pieces of screen to keep the soil from coming out. Water lilies and other aquatic plants generally need to spread *out* more than *down:* Pots for submerged plants and small floating-leaved plants can be as shallow as 4 inches. Use containers that are between 7 and 9 inches deep for most plants.

For water lilies and lotuses, the proper size container depends on the cultivar

of water lily and, to a lesser extent, the size of the pond. Larger containers encourage larger plants that cover more of the water's surface with their leaves. They also extend the amount of time before repotting is required. A $17 1/2$-quart container accommodates a water lily or a small lotus, while a 19-quart container provides space for one large or two small water lilies or a full-size lotus. Containers as large as 48 quarts are available; these are ideal for lotuses and large water lilies.

Most water gardeners grow marginal and floating-leaved plants in containers because they help to keep these vigorous spreaders under control. Place containers on marginal shelves, sink them to the rim in the soil of a bog garden, or set them directly in the water propped on stacks of bricks or weathered cinderblocks to achieve the proper water depth over the crowns of the plants. Containers in earth-bottomed ponds are useless for control purposes because the plants "jump" out of them. Moreover, most spread by seeds as well, so they can easily get out of control.

Generally, $3 1/2$- to 5-quart containers accommodate 1 or 2 marginals or floating-leaved plants; 9- to 10-quart containers provide room for 3 or 4 plants. Poke a few small holes in the bottom of containers for marginals and floating-leaved plants so that if the water level goes down for any reason, the plants won't dry out.

Potting Up and Setting Out. Fill containers with heavy garden soil and set the plants so shoot tips are just above the soil line. (Handle lotus tubers with special care, for they are very brittle and easily damaged.) Never use potting soil or topsoil that contains a large amount of compost or other organic matter. Ingredients such as perlite, vermiculite, composted bark, compost, and leaf mold float to the surface of the water when the pots are set in the garden. For containers that will be set directly in a water garden, fill to within an inch of the rim and add a $1/2$- to 1-inch layer of washed gravel on top of the soil. (Don't cover the growing tips of lotus tubers with gravel.) Gravel will discourage pond fish from digging into the soil and muddying the water. To wash gravel, make nail holes in an old plastic bucket, fill it with gravel, and rinse the gravel with a hose. An old colander works as well.

Before setting planted containers in the pool, thoroughly soak the soil with pond water to eliminate air pockets in the soil. (Do this at the pond's edge; water makes the containers much heavier.) This also reduces the amount of soil that will cloud the water when the plants are set into it (clouds of soil will settle in a day or so). Then set the containers in the water. Since the flooded containers are quite heavy, you will probably need a helper to move large ones. Once the containers are in the water, however, they are fairly easy to move into position if you keep them under water.

Set water lilies on the floor of the pond, spaced according to their estimated spread. Use stacks of bricks or weathered cinderblocks to raise containers of lotus, marginal, and floating-leaved plants to the proper water depth. Set lotus with 1 to 2 inches of water over the soil at first. After they produce aerial leaves, lower the containers to cover the soil surface with 4 to 12 inches of water. See the individual plant entries in chapter 4 for recommendations for marginals and floating-leaved plants. If you are introducing large fish, protect water lilies with plastic mesh, as described under "Growing Submerged Plants," below. Once the plants begin growing, you can rearrange them as necessary.

Growing Submerged Plants. Since submerged plants use their roots primarily as anchors and as a means to overwinter, they don't need to be potted in soil. Plan on 6 square inches of pot surface per each bunch (6 stems) of plants. To plant, fill pots or small tubs with washed sand to an inch below the rim. Rinse off the plants, which are generally sold in bunches, with a hose, and press them into the sand about 2 inches deep, either individually or an entire bunch at a time. Top-dress the sand with an inch of washed gravel. *Never fertilize submerged plants.* Note that submerged plants are sometimes grown in containers of gravel alone, but they will not survive snow-belt winters when planted in this manner.

Lower the containers gently into the water — water that is 1 to 2 feet over the gravel is best. For best results, spread the pots around the garden, keeping them away from areas that will be shaded by water lilies or other plants.

Fish eat the leaves of submerged plants, and newly planted pots may need protection, especially if your fish are large. To protect them, make domed "baskets" out of plastic mesh (sold by garden centers as bird netting; water garden suppliers sell mesh as well as baskets for plants). Simply wrap the mesh around the pots, fold it over on top, and secure it with a plastic holdfast. The plant stems grow out of the protective basket, and the fish will nibble on them, but the base of the plant is protected. To propagate most submerged plants, simply break off lengths of stem and pot them up.

FISH FOR A WATER GARDEN

Goldfish, koi, and other types of pond fish add movement, color, and entertainment value to a water garden. They also play a crucial role in the garden's ecosystem. On the plus side, fish eat mosquito larvae and other insects. However, too many fish in a water garden is the most common cause of green water. Overstocking leads to excess fish waste and fish food, providing single-celled algae with an abundance of nutrients. In severe cases, too many fish and too much decomposing organic matter in the water reduce the oxygen available. The first indication of a problem may be fish gasping for air at the surface. Large fish generally succumb to low oxygen conditions first. See "Troubleshooting" on page 112 for problems to watch out for and effective solutions.

In a new garden, stock up to 1 inch of goldfish (including the tail) per 5 gallons of water. If you are introducing koi, only stock a maximum of $^{1}/_{2}$ inch of koi per five gallons. These recommendations assume all fish are under 6 inches long; stock at a lower level if you are adding fish larger than that size. It's fine to stock at half the suggested maximum rate. Spring and fall are the best times to add fish.

Goldfish *(Carassius auratus)* come in several forms suitable for water gardens. Comets, which have long single tails and a rich golden orange color, are the most common. Some are spotted with or change to pearly white. Shubunkins resemble comets but are mottled with orange, black, blue-gray, red, and silvery white. Japanese fantails and calico fantails both have elaborate double tails and short, rounded bodies. Japanese fantails are solid red-orange in color or may be marked with or change to pearly white. Calico fantails have the same colors as shubunkins. In a large pool, comets and shubunkins can reach 10 to 12 inches in length; fantails may reach 6 to 8 inches.

Koi *(Cyprinus carpio)* are stunning fish that were first bred in Japan. They come in an array of colors and patterns, including solids such as silvery white, lemon yellow, and red-orange, and patterned fish in many variations, including white, red-orange, and black. Butterfly koi resemble regular koi but have extra-

---

Natural Mosquito Controls

Fish control mosquito larvae in a water garden, especially if they are still slightly hungry after feeding time. Floating Mosquito Dunks or Bactimos Briquettes are an easy organic way to control larvae in unstocked pools as well as any other shallow-water area. These contain *Bacillus thuringiensis israelensis,* a form of BT effective against mosquito larvae and black fly larvae. Each donut-shaped pellet lasts 30 days and treats 100 square feet of water surface.

Goldfish and koi quickly learn to come to the surface for food if you feed them on a regular schedule. Feeding time provides a good opportunity to examine fish for problems such as diseases and pests. See "Troubleshooting" on page 112 if you suspect a problem.

long fins. While exhibition-quality koi can be quite expensive, pool-quality ones are attractive and relatively inexpensive. Koi can reach 2 feet or more in length and are not good choices for small pools (under 25 square feet).

In a planted pool with large koi, use large containers, 2 feet or more in diameter, with 4 to 6 inches of water over the soil surface. (Set containers on stacks of bricks or weathered cinderblocks.) Koi are fond of tender young foliage, but are reluctant to expose themselves to predators in such shallow water. Also, feeding koi generously helps provide passive protection to tender foliage. Koi fanciers generally maintain water gardens with a minimum number of plants and extensive filtration to show off their prime fish to best advantage.

To introduce fish to a water garden, float the plastic bags containing the fish on the water for 15 to 20 minutes to equalize the temperature. If the weather is sunny, place a sheet of damp newspaper over the bag to shade it. Then open the bag and let water come into it from the surrounding pool before releasing the fish. Newly introduced fish may take a few days to settle in and begin eating. Newly introduced koi may jump out of the water; stretching netting across the pool surface for a few days can prevent this.

While most water gardeners enjoy feeding their fish, in a properly stocked pool they will find plenty of food without any supplemental feeding whatsoever. If you decide to feed, provide only what the fish can eat within about 3 to 5 minutes. (Their appetites increase with the water temperature.) Establish a schedule that is convenient for you; feed daily, twice a day, a few times a week, or not at all. Goldfish and koi quickly learn to come to the surface at the appointed time if you feed them regularly. Stop feeding in fall when water temperatures drop below 45°F and don't resume feeding until spring, when temperatures go above that level.

Although goldfish and koi will breed in a water garden, don't make the mistake of trying to save all the baby fish, called fry, by providing extra rations. The inevitable overpopulation that occurs leaves you with green water and potentially unhealthy conditions. Give excess fish to friends with new water gardens or use them to stock a new garden of your own. *Do not* release them into natural waterways where they could upset the existing ecological balance. In some areas, releasing them is illegal.

SPRING AND SUMMER CARE

Once it is planted and stocked, a water garden requires surprisingly little care. For most gardeners, the season starts in spring, when growth resumes, and finishes up in late fall, when the pump is turned off and the pool is winterized. In mild climates — Zones 8 or 9 through 11 — the garden becomes dormant briefly or not at all in winter. Gardeners in those zones should keep pumps running year-round and perform fall and winter maintenance tasks at or just before the coldest part of the year.

Here is a rundown of the seasonal care your garden may require.

Maintaining Equipment. Return pumps to the water and start filters in spring when the water begins warming up (45° to 50°F) and the fish become active. To give biological filters a spring boost, inoculate with beneficial bacteria, available from water garden suppliers. Depending on the type of filter in your pool, you need to clean it out daily, weekly, or monthly. Also clear the water intake on the pump regularly; it can become clogged with debris. If the pump is recirculating a reduced volume of water, it is a sign that the pump screen, volute (blade housing), or tubing needs cleaning.

Adding Water. Whenever the water level is down a few inches, fill the garden with a hose. Remember that newly added water from a municipal supplier needs to be treated for chlorine, chlorine dioxide, or chloramine. Calculate how many gallons you are adding and treat according to the directions in "Testing and Treating the Water" at the beginning of this chapter.

If the water level goes down quickly, you may have a leak. See "Troubleshooting" on page 112 for techniques for finding it.

Pinching, Pruning, and Thinning. Pinch yellowing leaves and spent flowers off water lily plants whenever you spot them. Try to pinch the stems off as close to the crown of the plant as possible, either by wading into the water or reaching from the edge. Specially designed long-handled pruners are also available.

Thin, pull up, or cut back marginals and floating-leaved plants as necessary throughout the season to keep them from spreading too far. Floating-leaved plants can cover the entire surface if not thinned when needed. Remove excess free-floating plants with a net; a rake works well for floating-leaved plants. Submerged plants also may need to be thinned out so they do not clog the water. Frequent short weeding sessions leave the garden looking its best and keep this task from seeming overwhelming. Give tadpoles, dragonfly larvae, and other pond inhabitants time to escape before placing thinnings on the compost pile.

Fertilizing Plants. Both water lilies and lotuses are heavy feeders. Use fish-safe water garden fertilizer pellets according to directions. In general, for best bloom, feed water lilies once a month (twice monthly when temperatures are over 75°F) and lotuses twice a month from the time they begin growing in spring until one

month before the first fall frost. Special pelleted fertilizer is available, and pellets should be stuck into the soil according to package directions. (If pellets become crushed, wrap them in a scrap of newspaper before putting them into the soil.)

Dividing and Propagating Plants. Reduced bloom and overcrowded leaves that stick out of the water are signs that water lilies need dividing. In Zone 8 and warmer, water lilies may need dividing annually, but in cooler areas they may only need dividing every two to three years. Factors besides climate that affect how often a plant needs dividing are soil, container size, plant variety, fertilizing, amount of direct sun, stillness of the water, and plant pests. Lotuses generally need dividing every five or so years; more often south of Zone 8. Plants in larger containers require dividing less frequently. In Zones 9 to 11, divide tropical water lilies when they appear crowded; in cooler zones, they should be replaced annually or overwintered indoors. Some gardeners go years and years between dividing water lilies, lotuses, and marginals, but this means the pond will require a major cleaning and dividing operation at some future date.

Spring is the best time to divide both water lilies and lotuses. Water lilies can also be divided anytime in summer, although flowering is reduced for several weeks while plants become reestablished. Lotuses, on the other hand, can only be divided in spring (about the time their first leaves are halfway to the water surface) because the fleshy, banana-shaped tubers required for success disappear over the summer.

To divide water lilies, lift the containers and set them in a shady spot. Gently remove the plants from the containers and wash the soil off the rhizomes. At first you'll see a tangle of rough, cylindrical, potato-like rhizomes, but if you look carefully, you'll see healthy growing tips and sections of rhizomes that will make vigorous new plants. Cut the rhizomes into 4- to 6-inch sections, each with a healthy growing point, or eye. (Eyes may have a cluster of leaves or may simply look like eyes on a potato.) Then replant as you would a new water lily. Pot up extra sections if you have space for them or give them to friends who would appreciate a start. (You can also pot up the small, thumb-size "eyes," each with a section of rhizome, in small pots under 4 to 6 inches of water, if you need additional plants.) Discard excess portions of the rhizome on the compost pile and set the water lilies back in the pool.

Crowded leaves that stick up above the water's surface are one sign that this hardy water lily ('Virginia') may need dividing soon. This plant still seems to be blooming well, however, as evidenced by the number of flowers and buds showing above the surface.

Lift lotus containers in the same manner and divide the plants into sections of tuber with a growing point and two or three nodes or joints where rootlets come out. Handle the divisions very carefully and replant as you would a new lotus. Discard any tubers that break. Another option is to pull out some tubers to thin the plants, leaving enough tubers in to regenerate the stand in that container. Keep in mind that tubers pulled out without special care to the brittle growing point have little chance of being established in a new container.

Divide hardy marginals and floating-leaved plants in spring or early summer to reduce clump size or for propagation. Plants may be divided every two or three years, and probably annually south of Zone 8. Simply dig the entire clump or lift the container and divide it as you would any perennial. Discard old, woody portions of the roots and replant the youngest, most vigorous ones.

When water lilies and other plants cover the entire surface of the water, eliminating open areas where water can sparkle in the sunlight, it's a signal to thin plants and clean out the pond. Reducing the surface coverage in this pond to about 60 percent will restore much of its appeal.

Controlling Pests. A variety of insects and animals attack aquatic plants. See "Troubleshooting" on page 112 for symptoms and controls.

Cleaning Out the Pool. Every few years, it's a good idea to drain the garden and spruce it up with a thorough clean-out if there is an inch or more of debris or sludge on the bottom. It's best to start the process in fall, to remove debris from the pond before winter ice traps toxic gases from decaying organic matter in the water. An early spring clean-out is the next best option, when water temperatures are in the 50s. Avoid cleaning ponds out in summer, when heat causes stress for fish, scavengers, plants, and you.

Drain the pool using a pump or siphon. Direct the water to flower beds or shrub borders; avoid draining it into a neighbor's yard. Remove plants and set them in a shady place. Cover stems and foliage with damp newspaper to prevent them from drying out. Fill clean buckets, tubs, a child's swimming pool, or plastic garbage cans with water from the pool for fish, tadpoles, snails, and other pool residents. When all but a few inches of water are left in the pool, scoop out fish and other creatures and place them in their temporary quarters in the shade. Use an aquarium pump with an airstone to provide oxygen, and cover the tops of the fish containers with screens or netting weighted down with bricks to prevent fish (especially koi and golden orfe) from jumping out.

Clean out the bottom of the pool, but leave the mosslike algae clinging to the pond sides to speed the balancing process. Removing it removes the beneficial microorganisms that are essential to a balanced ecosystem. Then begin to refill the garden. This is also a good time to repot water lilies and other plants if they are crowded. Treat the water for chlorine or other additives and replace the plants.

While the pond is filling, compare the new water temperature to the water temperature in the containers holding the fish. Temperature shock is the most common cause of fish death during cleaning. (Overcrowding in temporary holding containers is the second.) If the temperatures are within 3°F of each other, return the fish to the pond. *Do not* add the old water, which by now contains unwanted ammonia. If the temperatures differ by more than 3°F, slowly add fresh water from the hose to the temporary containers, lowering the temperature about 1°F per 4 to 5 minutes. When the water in the containers is within 2°F of the pond water temperature, place the fish in the newly filled pond.

FALL AND WINTER CARE

In late summer or early fall, the season in the water garden begins to wind down. Tropical water lilies bloom for 1 to 2 months after hardy types have stopped blooming, but when water temperatures dip into the 50s, even the tropicals stop blooming. When that happens, it's time to begin thinking about preparing the water garden for winter. (Gardeners in frost-free zones continue spring and summer care throughout the year; plants simply grow more slowly or stop growing altogether during the coolest part of the winter.)

Winterizing Plants. Hardy water lilies can be left in the pool over winter in Zones 3 through 11 unless the water garden will freeze to the depth of their crowns. Cut back the stems and floating pads, then set them on the bottom of the pool if they aren't there already. Also cut back lotuses and set them on the pool floor over winter. If the garden is shallow and there is a chance it will freeze to the bottom, move hardy lilies and lotuses to a cool, frost-free garage or basement. (Move fish indoors to an aerated aquarium covered with a screen in this case as well.) Wrap the plants, still in their containers, in damp newspaper and then in a plastic bag to keep them moist. Check regularly through the winter to make sure they stay damp. Return plants to the garden at the appropriate time in spring, when the pond is ice-free at least in the afternoon.

Cut back the foliage of marginals to just above the water line and the floating-leaved plants an inch or so above the soil container soon after they are cut down by frost. Cattails are an exception; enjoy them waving in the winter wind and then cut them above the water line in spring when new shoots emerge from the soil.

Overwintering Tropicals. Tropical plants can be left in the garden to freeze at the end of the season, but some are easy to overwinter. For information on overwintering tropical marginals, see the individual plant entries in chapter 4. Tropical water lilies produce tubers that can be kept from one season to the next. A month after the first killing frost, lift the containers of tropicals out of the water. Dump out the plants and wash the soil off the roots to reveal the hard tubers. Air-dry the tubers at room temperature for two days, then brush off any remaining soil and remove any remaining roots. Store the tubers in a cool (55°F), dark place in a jar of distilled water. (A cool but frost-free closet is fine.) Pot up the tubers in spring, two months before water temperatures will reach 70°F. Sprout them in a pan of water in a sunny window, then repot them in a 4-inch container covered with 2 to 4 inches of water before returning them to the pond when the water temperature is a minimum of 70°F.

Maintaining Equipment. Pull the pump (never by the power cord) and disconnect filters in late fall, before ice forms. Check the manufacturer's recommendations for annual maintenance and clean all equipment. Store the pump over the winter in a container of water that will not freeze. Replace worn filter pads.

Removing Leaves. An excess of decomposing leaves in the water can reduce oxygen levels, so it's best to avoid a buildup in fall. If lots of leaves find their way into the water, scoop them out daily with a net, or stretch plastic netting over the water's surface, then gather it up every few days along with the leaves. Alternatively, use a skimmer to remove them from the water's surface or use a leaf vacuum to remove them from the bottom.

Preventing Ice. Even though water lilies and fish are hardy, a solid layer of ice over the pool in winter poses problems. Gases in the water need to be able to escape, and fish need oxygen. Ice covering the water prevents this normal exchange of gases. (Submerged plants are dormant in winter and won't release oxygen.) The easiest way to keep the water from freezing is to float an electric deicer in the water from late fall through early spring. These devices, designed to keep an ice-free area on the pond, have a thermostat and run only enough to keep a portion of the water surface a few degrees above freezing. They are available from water garden suppliers as well as hardware and farm stores that carry livestock supplies. Plug them into a circuit with a ground fault interrupter. (Setting a pan full of boiling water on the ice will not melt a temporary hole in an emergency, since the water freezes before it melts through the ice.) In Zones 8 and farther south, where pools rarely freeze for more than three days, ice is not really a problem. Never break the ice forcibly, as it can harm fish.

Chapter 4:

Plants for a
Water Garden

Fun frustration is perhaps the best way to sum up the enjoyable task of selecting plants for a water garden. There are hundreds of water lilies to choose
from, each more beautiful than the last, as well as a wealth of dazzling lotuses
and striking marginal and floating-leaved plants for shallow water areas.

Although it's tempting to include one of each type of plant that appeals to
you, moderation is the key to success: Overplanting affects both the appearance
and the health of your pond. One of the most appealing aspects of a garden pool
is the sight of water glittering in the sun. Expanses of still water also provide a
reflective mirror for the sky, water lilies, and the surrounding plantings. Overplanting inevitably leads to foliage completely covering the pool's surface, oblit-
erating reflections along with the sight of the water itself. Too many plants can
also lead to an excess of decomposing matter in the water, causing unhealthy conditions for fish and other pond life.

*Contrasting foliage color, texture, and shape create a striking
combination in this grouping of plants surrounding a delightful
mermaid fountain pouring water back into the garden.*

DECIDING WHAT TO BUY

So how can you settle on a few plants when the choices are so vast and tempting? You'll find that your garden and landscape will provide a wealth of ideas on precisely which plants to buy if you take a moment to look at them. Use the ideas below to get you started, and see "Planting, Stocking, and Clear Water" on page 56 to determine how many plants your water garden will accommodate.

Repeat Colors. Repetition of colors, as well as shapes and textures, is a powerful design tool that can be used to link a water garden visually to the larger landscape, thus creating a unified design. For this reason, water lilies, lotuses, or marginal plants with flowers in colors that figure prominently in another part of the landscape are often a good choice. Remember that water lilies will be blooming at the height of summer, so base your choices on the colors that predominate in your garden from June through August. For example, a yellow water lily such as 'Chromatella' will pick up the colors of cheerful 'Lemon Gem' marigolds in a nearby flower bed. Water lily 'Pink Opal', which has deep pink flowers and bronze-hued leaves, may be the perfect accent for a Japanese maple such as 'Bloodgood', which has red-purple leaves.

Repeat Foliage Types. The texture, color, and shape of foliage can also serve as a powerful unifier when repeated throughout a garden. The graceful leaves of cattails or spike rushes can be used to repeat the texture of ornamental grasses, for example. Or golden-leaved creeping Jenny (*Lysimachia nummularia* 'Aurea') can be used to repeat the color of a clump of variegated or golden-leaved hostas.

Plan for Foliage Interest. Foliage can also be used as an eye-catching accent. A clump of variegated sweet flag (*Acorus calamus* 'Variegatus') makes a handsome accent at the edge of a pond, for example. You can also group several plants with contrasting foliage types and colors to add interest to a water garden. For real foliage drama, consider using some of the tropical marginals. A clump of dwarf papyrus *(Cyperus isocladus)* or Egyptian paper reed *(C. papyrus)* looks like a fireworks display in foliage; the huge leaves of taros (*Colocasia* spp.) lend a tropical look to a garden.

Tropical water lilies, along with a mix of marginal and floating-leaved plants, crowd around the base of a charming piped statue, filling a corner of this water garden with colorful flowers and handsome foliage. Plenty of water is left uncovered to reflect the sky, the flowers, and the statue.

Consider Color Themes. One of the easiest ways to narrow down your choices is to design with a color scheme in mind—hot-colored yellows and oranges or a cool pink-and-blue mix, for example. For an all-white garden, consider classic white water lily 'Virginia' combined with lotus 'Alba Grandiflora', Siberian iris 'White Swirl', and a white-flowered form of pickerel rush *(Pontederia cordata)*. Tropical water lilies make it easy to design a garden with a blue-and-purple theme. Pair them with blue Siberian or Louisiana irises and pickerel rush.

Choose the Right-size Plants. Select plants that are compatible with the size of your pond. The largest hardy lilies will spread to cover as much as 18 square feet and may take up too much room in a small pond, especially if you want more than one lily. Instead, look for plants recommended for small pools. Two of the smallest are hardy lily 'Helvola', which spreads to $1^{1}/_{2}$ square feet; tropical water lily *Nymphaea colorata* ranges from 1 to 6 square feet in spread and can be grown with just 3 inches of water over the crown. Tulip lotus (*Nelumbo nucifera* 'Shirokunshi') and lotus 'Momo Botan' are ideal for growing in containers in small ponds. Look for compact marginals, too. For example, fill a container with dwarf cattail *(Typha minima)*, which is 2 feet tall, instead of common cattail *(T. latifolia)*, which reaches 7 feet.

For best effect in a large pond, select wide-spreading water lilies and plant them in large containers (more than 15 inches across) so they can attain full size. Plant marginals in large containers, too, and plant three or more of each type to create bold drifts of plants. Repeating clumps of the same plant around the pool will help unify the design—this is a good way to use repetition in a small pool as well. Restricting plants to small containers and planting a single specimen of many different plants can lead to a jumbled, unsatisfying appearance, whatever size pond you have.

Select Plants for Your Growing Conditions. There's no point in lying to yourself about how much sun your water garden receives—the plants you select won't be fooled, even if you are. The ideal site receives a minimum of five to six hours of direct sun daily. If yours receives sun for only part of the day, select water lilies that bloom in partial sun: There are both hardy and tropical lilies that flower with between three and five hours of sun daily. A few, including hardy lily

'Helvola' and tropical 'Dauben', bloom with as little as two hours of direct sun daily. Avoid lotuses altogether in a pond that receives less than full sun. Fortunately for gardeners with little sun, a variety of marginal plants — especially tropicals — thrive in partial shade.

Consider Style. The style of garden you have may affect your plant choices as well. A formal pool surrounded by a brick terrace may look best with symmetrical plantings — a pair of water lilies and matching clumps of iris or other marginal plants in each corner, for example. Formal-looking clumps of cannas may fit in better than more casual-looking cattails. Informal pools lend themselves to asymmetrical groupings of mixed water lilies and marginal plants. Try clustering three to five different marginals on one side of the pond and balancing them with a smaller grouping on the other. For a wildlife pool, you may decide to stick with native North American plants only.

Plan for Clear Water. Whatever you do, don't scrimp on submerged plants: Of all the plants you select, these have the greatest effect on how clear the water will be. Water lilies and other floating-leaved plants also help ensure clear water — between 60 and 70 percent of the surface of a 100-square-foot pond should be covered with floating foliage. The water in a newly filled and planted pond will probably turn green, but if you have planted the right mix of plants, the water will begin to clear within four to six weeks as they become established. Review the "Proper Planting Proportions" on page 58 to determine how many bunches of submerged plants you need before you place your order.

SUBMERGED PLANTS

All too often unappreciated, submerged plants are the workhorses of the water garden. Not only do they provide shelter and shade for baby fish (or fry) and food for adult fish, they also help control the algae that turn pond water a murky green if left unchecked. Submerged plants accomplish this feat by competing directly with algae for light and food. Unlike most plants, which take up nutrients through their roots, submerged plants absorb nutrients through their leaves. By taking nutrients derived from fish waste and minerals directly out of the water,

they help starve out algae and keep the water clear. Sometimes referred to as oxygenators, submerged plants release oxygen into the water in daytime, but they release carbon dioxide at night. Fish contribute carbon dioxide, too, while consuming oxygen. In general, this doesn't pose a problem, but in a heavily stocked pond overgrown with submerged plants, too much carbon dioxide can build up at nighttime, especially when the water is warm, stressing or even killing the fish. During hot weather it is wise to oxygenate the water using a bubbler, waterfall, fountain, piped statuary, or an aerator (air pump).

Selecting Submerged Plants. Water garden suppliers offer a variety of species of submerged plants. See "Growing Submerged Plants" on page 61 for directions on planting and care. The following three are the most popular selections:

- *Egeria densa* / **Anacharis**

This North American native has branched stems with short dark green leaves. It bears tiny white flowers held just above the water's surface in summer. It is fast-growing; trim it back in midsummer, more than once if necessary, to keep it from taking over more than about one-third of your pond. Add the trimmings to the compost pile or use them as mulch. Zones 5 to 11.

- *Myriophyllum* **spp.** / **Water milfoil**

Milfoils produce branched stems with delicate, feathery foliage. They are so efficient at filtering out pond debris that the hairlike leaves can become brown-looking; if desired, simply shake the stems with your hand to dislodge the debris. Zones 4 to 11, depending on the species. Parrot's feather *(M. aquaticum)* is grown as a marginal or floating-leaved plant; for more on this species, see page 106.

- *Vallisneria americana* / **Wild celery**

Also commonly called eel grass or tape grass, this native North American species grows in grasslike clumps. The bright green leaves are gently curving and ribbonlike. Unlike other submerged plants, it spreads by stolons. To propagate it, break off individual plants that arise at the ends of the stolons and replant them.

WATER LILIES

Without doubt, water lilies are the jewels of the water garden. Often simply called lilies by water gardeners, they belong to the genus *Nymphaea* and provide one of the longest seasons of bloom of any garden plant. Hardy lilies are in bloom any time summer temperatures average in the 70s, with water temperatures above 60°F. Tropicals need several weeks of temperatures in the 80s to begin blooming, but they bloom later in fall than hardies. In the middle part of the country, that means flowers from roughly late May well into September. In Southern gardens they may bloom for six or seven months; nearly year-round in frost-free areas.

Flowers come in a rainbow of colors, and bloom size ranges from 2 or 3 inches to 10 or 12 inches. Blooms are semidouble or double and are borne on

Water lily 'Sultan' is a free-flowering cultivar that forms a healthy clump but won't take over even an earth-bottomed pond.

the water's surface or on stalks held above the water. Each flower generally lasts for three to four days. The round, floating leaves are handsome, too. Leaves are sometimes held an inch or more above the surface in very shallow water or when plants are crowded, indicating that it's time to divide. They may be bright to rich green, bronze or maroon (especially new leaves), or mottled with purple-brown or bronze or variegated. By shading the water, the leaves also help control algae and shelter fish.

Despite their exotic appearance, water lilies are extremely easy to grow. They bloom best in full sun—a *minimum* of 5 to 6 hours of direct sun daily is best, although there are cultivars that flower in dappled shade with as few as 2 hours of direct sun. As far as water lilies are concerned, however, the sunnier the site the better. Plants in shadier sites inevitably bloom less than ones that are growing in full sun.

Hardy or Tropical? Actually, the answer to this question may be "both," since both hardies and tropicals have their advantages. To ensure abundant flowers, a long season of bloom, and a wide range of shapes and colors, consider planting some of each.

Selecting Plant Size. The spread of both hardy and tropical lilies is measured in the number of square feet the leaves cover in a pond. Spread varies considerably from plant to plant: Large plants can cover between 9 and 18 square feet of water surface, while the smallest ones can be kept to as little as 1 square foot. Soil container size plays a role in controlling the spread of the plants, with smaller containers helping to keep plants at the smallest end of the range. For example, when planted in a $3^1/_2$-quart soil container, tropical water lily 'Dauben' might cover 4 or 5 square feet of water surface. When planted in a 19-quart soil container, the same plant could cover three to four times as much area.

When grown in earth-bottomed ponds, some water lilies eventually cover the entire surface of the water because their fleshy rhizomes colonize every available square foot. Ask your dealer about which lilies will spread in earth-bottomed ponds: *Nymphaea odorata* varieties such as *N. odorata gigantea,* plants with *N. tuberosa*-type rootstocks, and tropical species in their native climates will spread. There are many water lily hybrids that stay in clumps like iris; although these

Flowers for Cutting

Many water lilies make fine cut flowers. For longest life, pick them the day they open by reaching into the pool and pinching or cutting the stem about a foot under the water. Never tug at the stems, for this can disturb the plants. To ensure that flowers remain open, hold them right-side up by the stem and use a lighted candle to drip a drop of wax between each petal. The liquid wax quickly hardens into a wedge at the base of each petal, making closing impossible. When arranging the flowers, place hardy water lilies in water to within an inch of the flower. Arrange tropicals in water to within 3 inches of the base. Keep cut water lilies out of direct sun. They last for 3 or 4 days.

will multiply, they won't take over. Planting water lilies in containers to control their spread doesn't work in an earth-bottomed pond because they "jump" out of their containers and continue spreading unchecked.

HARDY WATER LILIES

Hardy water lilies can be grown outdoors year-round in USDA Zones 3 through 11. In the north, they die down in fall and return each spring, with leaves appearing before the flowers. In frost-free zones, they remain evergreen and bloom year-round, year after year, although the flowers become scarce during the coldest months. Hardy lilies require still water and prefer between 6 and 18 inches of water over the top of the rootstock.

Flowers, which usually float on the water's surface, come in white, pink, peach, salmon, red, and yellow, as well as so-called changeable apricot-colored types, which are a yellowish color when they open and turn reddish as they mature. Blooms open during the day at around 9:00 A.M. and close in the afternoon between 3:00 and 5:00 P.M. Variations occur depending on the cultivar, temperature, age of flower, and amount of sun. Flowers may not be fully open during cloudy, dark weather. Many hardy lilies are fragrant, and most have a showy cluster of yellow stamens in the center of the bloom.

Hardy water lily 'Virginia'

▪ White Hardy Lilies

'**Hermine**'. Ivory white 4- to 5-inch flowers. Round, bright green leaves. Blooms with as little as 3 hours of direct sun. Spreads 4 to 12 square feet.

'**Perry's Double White**'. Free-flowering cultivar with cup-shaped 4- to 5-inch white blooms. Round, deep green leaves. Good for all sizes of gardens, from tubs to large pools. Spreads 4 to 12 square feet.

'**Virginia**'. Showy 6- to 7-inch double white flowers produced over a long blooming season. Green leaves blotched purple at the edges; new leaves are heavily marked with purple. Spreads 9 to 18 square feet.

'**Virginialis**'. Classic free-flowering cultivar with pure white 4- to 5$\frac{1}{2}$-inch blooms produced over a long blooming season. New leaves are purple-bronze, maturing to green. Grows in up to 3 feet of water. Spreads 9 to 18 square feet.

Hardy water lily
'Pink Beauty'

■ Pink Hardy Lilies

'Arc en Ciel'. Fragrant, pastel pink $4^1/_2$- to $5^1/_2$-inch flowers. Handsome olive green leaves variegated with pink, cream, bronze-red, and purple. Spreads 9 to 18 square feet.

'Marliacea Carnea' (*N.* × *marliacea* 'Carnea'). Very pale pink, cup-shaped 4- to 5-inch blooms, darker pink near the center. Fragrant. New leaves purplish, maturing to green. Very free-flowering and a good cut flower. Good for small to large pools with from 10 inches to 3 feet of water over the crowns. Blooms well with as little as 3 hours of direct sun daily. Spreads 4 to 12 square feet.

'Masaniello'. Rose-pink 4- to 5-inch flowers with pale pink to white outer petals. Fragrant. Bright green leaves. Will bloom well with as little as 3 hours of direct sun daily. Spreads 6 to 12 square feet.

'Pink Beauty'. Cup-shaped 4- to 5-inch pink flowers borne in abundance. Green leaves. Spreads 6 to 12 square feet. Sometimes listed as 'Fabiola' and 'Luciana'.

'Rosy Morn'. Showy 6- to 7-inch tulip-shaped flowers with deep pink inner petals and pale pink outer ones. Fragrant. New leaves purplish, maturing to green. Dependable bloomer. Spreads 6 to 12 square feet.

'Pink Opal'. Cup-shaped 3- to 4-inch fragrant, deep pink blooms held above the water's surface. Bronze-green to green leaves. Will spread widely in earth-bottomed ponds. Spreads 6 to 12 square feet.

*Hardy water lily
'James Brydon'*

■ Red Hardy Lilies

'Attraction'. Deep garnet red 6- to 8-inch blooms. Bronzy new leaves mature to green. Blooms well with as little as 3 hours of direct sun. Although some red lilies do poorly in warm climates, 'Attraction' performs well even in Zones 8 to 11. Spreads 6 to 18 square feet.

'Ellisiana'. Brilliant rose-red 3- to 4-inch blooms. Bright green leaves. Good for tubs and small gardens, but stops blooming in very hot weather and is best in Zones 3 to 7. Spreads 4 to 12 square feet.

'Frobeli'. Burgundy-red $4^1/_2$- to 5-inch blooms on compact plants. Bronze-green new leaves maturing to green. Good for small gardens. Best in Zones 3 to 7. Spreads 4 to 12 square feet.

'Giverny Red' (*N. × laydekeri* 'Fulgens'). Rose-red 4- to 5-inch blooms with yellow centers that hold their color even in Zones 8 to 11. Round, medium green leaves. Will bloom well with as little as 3 hours of direct sun daily. Spreads 4 to 12 square feet.

'James Brydon'. Rich rose-red 4- to 5-inch blooms with orange-yellow anthers. New leaves blotched with purple-brown, maturing to green. Good for small tub gardens to large pools. Best in Zones 3 to 8. Spreads 6 to 12 square feet.

*Hardy water lily
'Charlene Strawn'*

■ Yellow Hardy Lilies

'Charlene Strawn'. Fragrant 4- to 5-inch yellow flowers held above the water's surface. New leaves mottled, maturing to green. Blooms with as little as 3 hours of direct sun daily. Spreads 6 to 12 square feet.

'Chromatella' (*N.* × *marliacea* 'Chromatella'). Pale yellow, cup-shaped 3½- to 4½-inch blooms with dark yellow anthers and stamens. Leaves mottled with purple. Dependable and long-blooming. Good for tub gardens and pools small and large. Will not spread excessively in earth-bottomed ponds. Blooms well with as little as 3 hours of direct sun daily. Spreads 4 to 12 square feet.

'Helvola'. Tiny 1½- to 3-inch yellow flowers. Diminutive leaves heavily mottled with dark purple. Blooms with as little as 2 hours of direct sun and can be grown in a 12-inch diameter bowl. Sometimes called 'Yellow Pygmy'. Spreads 1 to 1½ square feet.

'Joey Tomocik'. Rich deep yellow 4- to 5-inch flowers borne in abundance. Green leaves. Spreads 6 to 12 square feet.

'Texas Dawn'. Showy, pure yellow 5- to 6-inch blooms borne over a long season. Blooms held above the water's surface on strong stems. Green leaves with soft brown blotches. Blooms with as little as 3 hours of direct sun daily. Hardy to Zone 5. Spreads 9 to 18 square feet.

Changeable water lily 'Comanche'

■ Changeable Hardy Lilies

'Charlie's Choice'. Coppery orange 3- to 4-inch flowers deepen to orange-red as they mature. Green leaves with brown flecks. Blooms with as little as 3 hours of direct sun daily. Spreads 4 to 12 square feet.

'Comanche'. Yellow 5- to 6-inch flowers with red flecks change to red-flecked golden orange on the second day and deep orange-bronze-red on the third. Bronze-green leaves flecked with purple. Blooms with as little as 3 hours of direct sun daily. Spreads 6 to 12 square feet.

'Paul Hariot'. Free-flowering changeable with 3- to 4-inch flowers emerging apricot-orange and maturing to pinkish orange. Handsome green foliage mottled with purple-brown. Blooms with as little as 3 hours of direct sun daily. Good for tubs or small to medium gardens. Spreads 4 to 12 square feet.

TROPICAL WATER LILIES

Tropical lilies are actually frost-tender perennials; they bloom year-round in frost-free zones but are killed by repeated freezing temperatures—in other words, north of Zones 10 to 11. In Zones 3 to 9 they are generally grown as annuals and replaced each year. Growing tropicals makes it easy to change the color scheme of the garden every year, although they can also be overwintered indoors and replanted outdoors each spring. See "Overwintering Tropicals" on page 70 for details on keeping these plants over the winter.

Tropicals can be planted outdoors once minimum water temperature reaches 70°F, and they begin blooming after they've received 2 to 3 weeks of temperatures in the 80s. Like hardy lilies, they require still water and prefer between 6 and 18 inches of water over the rootstock. In Zone 8 they begin blooming in mid-April to early May, but in cooler zones the first flowers are delayed until early June. In areas with cool summers, such as the Pacific Northwest, tropicals rarely bloom well. In areas with warm summers, however, tropicals more than make up for the delay, because they are extremely free-flowering and continue blooming into fall, a month or more after the hardies have gone to bed for the season.

Tropical lilies are further divided into day- or night-flowering types. Day-bloomers open their flowers from about 9:00 A.M. to 3:00 or 5:00 P.M., just like hardy types. The flowers of night-blooming tropicals open after the sun goes down and remain open until late morning or early afternoon, depending on the cultivar, temperature, and light conditions. Night-blooming water lilies are especially good choices for gardeners who work all day and miss day-bloomers except on weekends. Both day- and night-blooming tropical water lilies hold their showy blooms on stalks well above the water's surface. The flowers of all day-bloomers are fragrant, often extremely so. The flowers of night-bloomers have a heavy, somewhat pungent but pleasing scent.

■ Night-blooming Tropicals

Night-blooming tropicals bloom best with 6 hours or more of sun per day, but flower with as little as 3 hours of direct sun.

Tropical night-blooming water lily 'Red Flare'

'**Emily Grant Hutchings**'. Free-flowering, fragrant pink cultivar with 5- to 7-inch blooms. Bronze-green leaves with slightly ruffled edges. Ideal for a medium to large pool. Spreads 9 to 18 square feet.

'**H. C. Haarstick**'. Rich rose-red 5- to 7-inch blooms with showy orange-red stamens in the center. Good fragrance. Large, deep green leaves. Spreads 9 to 18 square feet.

'**Jennifer Rebecca**'. Large, abundant 5- to 7-inch rich red flowers with pungent fragrance. Handsome red-brown leaves. Spreads 9 to 18 square feet.

'**Red Flare**'. Deep red 7- to 10-inch blooms held up to 12 inches above the water's surface. Red-bronze leaves. Very free-flowering. Good for medium to large pools. Spreads 9 to 18 square feet.

Tropical night-blooming water lily 'Wood's White Knight'

'Wood's White Knight'. Fragrant, white 5- to 7-inch blooms with deep yellow anthers. Rich green leaves. Very free-flowering. Spreads 9 to 18 square feet.

■ Day-blooming Tropicals

Day-blooming tropicals come in yellow, pink, rose-yellow, white, blue, purple, and blue-green. One characteristic unique to day-bloomers is that some cultivars have viviparous leaves. That means the leaves produce small plantlets that can be detached and used for propagation. Simply detach plantlets and press them into a pan of soil. Then set the pan in a few inches of water. As the plants grow, lower the plants, potting as necessary. Plantlets will begin blooming in as little as 90 days.

*Tropical day-blooming
water lily 'Dauben'*

■ Blue and Purple Tropical Lilies

'**Blue Beauty**'. Lilac-blue 5- to 6-inch flowers with yellow centers and a rich, sweet fragrance. New leaves speckled and blotched with purple-brown, maturing to green. Free-flowering. Spreads 9 to 18 square feet.

'**Blue Capensis**'. Handsome 5- to 6-inch, lilac-blue flowers with glowing dark yellow centers. Young leaves speckled with purple. Grows with 6 inches to as much as 3 feet of water over the crowns of the plants. Spreads 6 to 12 square feet.

'**Charles Thomas**'. Soft lilac- to sky-blue 5- to 6-inch flowers over a long season. Green leaves mottled with maroon and purple-brown. Viviparous. Blooms with as little as 3 hours of direct sun daily. Spreads 4 to 12 square feet.

'**Dauben**'. Pale blue, starry 4- to 5-inch flowers with pale yellow centers, turning to nearly white on third day of bloom. Green leaves. Very viviparous. Blooms in as little as 2 hours of direct sun daily. Can be grown in soil containers as small as $3^{1}/_{2}$ quarts. Spreads 4 to 12 square feet.

'**Margaret Mary**'. Deep violet-blue 5- to $6^{1}/_{2}$-inch flowers borne in abundance. Green leaves. Somewhat viviparous. A medium-size plant, but will grow in containers as small as 3¹/₂ quarts. Will bloom with as little as 3 hours of direct sun daily. Spreads 6 to 12 square feet.

N. colorata. Small, free-blooming, tropical species lily with intense violet-blue 3- to 4-inch flowers. Green leaves. Suitable for tubs and small gardens, with as little as 6 inches of water over the rootstock. It can grow in only 3 inches of soil with a mere 3 inches of water over the crowns; in this case, 2 hours of shade during the hottest part of the day is best. Blooms with as little as 3 hours of sun daily. Spreads 4 to 6 square feet.

'**Panama Pacific**'. Violet-purple 4- to 5-inch cup-shaped blooms with deep yellow centers. Green leaves. Viviparous. Free-flowering and good in very small to large pools. Blooms with as little as 3 hours of direct sun daily. Spreads 4 to 18 square feet.

■ Pink and White Tropical Lilies

'**General Pershing**'. Showy 7- to 9-inch lavender-pink blooms borne in abundance. Olive green leaves mottled with maroon. Blooms open early in the morning and remain open until dusk over a long blooming season. Flowers with as little as 3 hours of direct sun daily. Spreads 9 to 18 square feet.

'**Pink Perfection**'. Striking, rosy pink 6- to 8-inch blooms borne in abundance. Green leaves heavily mottled with maroon. Prefers 6 to 18 inches of water over the crowns, but will grow in water to 3 feet deep. Blooms with as little as 3 hours of direct sun daily. Spreads 9 to 18 square feet.

'**Madame Ganna Walska**'. Violet-pink 5- to 6-inch flowers borne in abundance. Green leaves heavily mottled with maroon. Viviparous. Blooms with as little as 3 hours of direct sun daily. Spreads 4 to 12 square feet.

'**Marian Strawn**'. Pure white 6- to 8-inch flowers with yellow centers on stout stems above the water's surface. Green leaves speckled with purple. Blooms with as little as 3 hours of direct sun daily. Spreads 4 to 12 square feet.

'**White Delight**'. Fragrant, white 7- to 9-inch flowers with yellow centers borne in abundance. New leaves mottled with brownish purple, maturing to green. Spreads 9 to 18 square feet.

Tropical day-blooming water lily 'Albert Greenberg', foreground, growing with an unnamed rosy-purple tropical

■ Yellow and Sunset-colored Tropical Lilies

'Afterglow'. Colorful, fragrant 6- to 8-inch flowers featuring glowing yellow to orange petals. Green leaves. Free-flowering. Spreads 9 to 18 square feet.

'Albert Greenberg'. Showy 5- to 7-inch rosy yellow flowers with orange-pink petal tips. Green leaves mottled with purple. Very free-flowering and blooms well past the first early frost. Blooms with as little as 3 hours of direct sun daily. Spreads 9 to 18 square feet.

'Aviator Pring'. Deep yellow 5- to 7-inch blooms held well above the water. Green leaves. Fragrant and very free-flowering. Spreads 9 to 18 square feet.

'Golden West'. Salmon-pink 5- to 7-inch blooms mature to apricot orange. New leaves mottled with purple, maturing to green. Very free-flowering. Spreads 6 to 12 square feet.

'Yellow Dazzler'. Lemon yellow 5- to 7-inch flowers with golden yellow centers borne in abundance. Green leaves speckled with purple. Blooms stay open an hour or two after other tropicals close. Blooms with as little as 3 hours of direct sun daily. Spreads 9 to 18 square feet.

LOTUSES

Dramatic summer flowers and handsome foliage make lotuses (*Nelumbo* spp.) outstanding additions to a water garden. The single, semidouble, or double flowers are fragrant and come in white, pink, and yellow. Plants bloom for 6 to 8 weeks in midsummer and blooms open early in the morning and close in the afternoon. Each bloom usually lasts three days. When the petals fall, they leave cup-shaped seed pods that are attractive, especially when used in dried arrangements. The flowers are borne on tall stems among or above handsome, round, concave leaves. Leaves and flowers range from 1 to 7 feet above the rootstock, depending on the cultivar. Before and during the time lotuses produce aerial leaves, they also bear floating pads. Lotus leaves never get wet; water beads up on them as it would on a freshly waxed surface.

Lotuses are hardy perennials in Zones 4 to 11, but require several weeks of summer temperatures in the 90s in order to bloom well. For this reason, they seldom perform satisfactorily in cool-summer regions such as the Pacific Northwest. Like water lilies, lotuses need a minimum of 5 or 6 hours of direct sun daily. They also require still water and should be planted with between 2 and 4 inches of water above the rootstock. Grow full-size lotuses in 15-inch diameter containers or larger. Containers will not keep these vigorous spreaders under control in earth-bottomed ponds.

'Alba Grandiflora'. Pure white 6- to 8-inch fragrant blooms. Large, blue-green leaves. Flowers are held among the leaves and plants can reach 4 to 5 feet above the water's surface.

'Charles Thomas'. Fragrant, lavender-pink 5- to 7-inch flowers. Handsome round leaves. Good for containers and small pools. Plants range from 3 to 4 feet above the water's surface.

'Momo Botan'. Rose-pink 4- to 6-inch double flowers with yellow centers and sweet fragrance. Flowers last several days longer than most lotuses and may remain open until dusk or overnight. Handsome 1- to 1$^1/_2$-foot-diameter leaves. Plants range from 2 to 4 feet above the water's surface and are ideal for small water gardens or whiskey barrels.

Lotus 'Mrs. Perry D. Slocum'   *Lotus 'Charles Thomas'*

'**Mrs. Perry D. Slocum**'. Deep rose-pink 6- to 8-inch double blooms with rich fragrance change to creamy yellow. Blossoms are held above the round 18-inch-wide leaves. Plants range from 4 to 5 feet above the water's surface.

N. lutea. A native species, commonly called American lotus, with single 5- to 7-inch pale yellow flowers. Large, bowl-shaped leaves reach 2 feet in diameter, usually held 2 to 3 feet above the water. Flowers are usually held above the leaves, and plants can reach 5 feet high.

Tulip Lotus. (*N. nucifera* 'Shirokunshi'). White, tulip-shaped flowers on compact plants. Attractive round leaves. Plants reach 18 to 24 inches above the water's surface. Good for containers and small pools.

MARGINAL AND FLOATING-LEAVED PLANTS

Marginal and floating-leaved plants are invaluable for framing a water garden, softening its edges, and blending it into the garden as a whole. They can also add considerable texture, color, and drama. Grow them as specimens surrounded by water, combine them to highlight contrasting flowers and foliage, or create mass plantings for dramatic effect. Use the design ideas in "Deciding What to Buy" at the beginning of this chapter to help you select and design your own combinations of marginals.

Plants with floating leaves—both shallow-water types as well as free-floating plants—not only decorate the pond edges and the water, they are also part of the prescription for clear water. Along with water lilies and lotuses, they provide shade that helps control algae. Shade shelters fish. Some floating plants also filter nutrients out of the water with their roots, so they provide an additional algae-control function.

Most marginals grow in soil that remains constantly moist or in standing water up to a certain depth. In the encyclopedia entries below, you'll find water depth specified for each plant. Most are vigorous spreaders and should be kept in containers to keep them in bounds. Consider them invasive in all earth-bottomed ponds. Although planting in containers will easily control these plants in preformed or liner ponds, containers will not prevent spreading in earthen ones. For information on planting and caring for marginal and floating-leaved plants, see chapter 3.

Keep in mind that the soil *outside* a pool liner will be ordinary garden soil, generally not wet enough for these moisture-loving plants. For ideas on what to plant outside a liner, see "Water Garden Companions" on page 111. You'll also find ideas by studying the photos of gardens in this book or visiting local water gardens.

There are marginal plants for a range of exposures, from full sun to partial shade. In the entries below, full sun means a minimum of 5 to 6 hours of direct sun. Very light shade or partial sun means at least 3 hours of direct sun and dappled shade for the rest of the day. Partial shade means dappled shade, ideally with 1 hour of direct sun.

Floating Tropicals for Northern Gardens

Water hyacinth (Eichhornia crassipes)

Water hyacinths *(Eichhornia crassipes)* and water lettuce *(Pistia stratiotes)* are tropical species that make fine additions to northern water gardens. Both have roots that hang down into the water and are extremely efficient at keeping the water clear. In areas where they are hardy, however, these plants are menaces; they're outlawed in many states because they grow so vigorously that they clog waterways. Federal interstate commerce law prohibits shipment of water hyacinths from any state into any other state.

Water hyacinth, hardy in Zones 8 to 11, produces showy, hyacinth-like clusters of violet-blue flowers in summer. It floats on inflated, bladderlike leaf stalks. Water lettuce, hardy in Zones 9 to 11, produces floating, lettucelike rosettes of foliage that range from 4 inches to as much as 10 to 12 inches tall. Both are easy to grow as annuals and thrive in full sun to very light shade. To "plant," simply drop them into the water after it has reached 70°F. Scoop out excess plants and compost them through the summer to contain their spread. (Do not dispose of them in sewers or waterways.) You can let the plants be killed by hard frost or take a few indoors for overwintering. Simply keep them in a sunny spot in an aquarium or bucket of water with a 2- to 3-inch layer of soil at the bottom. The water depth should be such that the roots touch the soil.

■ *Acorus* spp. / Sweet Flag

Description: Sweet flags produce handsome strap-shaped or grassy leaves that are ideal for adding a vertical accent along the edge of a pond or in a bog garden. The dramatic clumps of semievergreen leaves are the plants' major attraction; the insignificant summer flowers are brown-green or white and catkinlike. The foliage of common sweet flag *(A. calamus)*, native to North America, resembles that of irises or cattails. Leaves are under 3/4 inches wide and 2 to 4 feet long. The leaves have a slightly sweet, spicy scent when crushed, and have been used as a strewing herb for centuries. The fragrant, fleshy rhizomes can be dried, ground, and added to potpourris as a fixative. Variegated sweet flag *(A. calamus* 'Variegatus') produces 2- to 3-foot-long leaves that are boldly striped with creamy white. It spreads more slowly than the species and is less fragrant. Grassy-leaved sweet flag *(A. gramineus)*, native to China and Japan, produces fountainlike clumps of narrow, arching, unscented leaves that reach 1 foot. Both variegated and dwarf cultivars are available. 'Variegata' has white-striped, foot-long leaves. 'Masamune' has creamy white variegation and reaches only 6 inches. 'Minimus' is all green and remains a diminutive 3 inches.

Culture: Sweet flags thrive in full sun to partial shade. Grow them in rich soil that remains constantly moist or in shallow water. *A. calamus* can be grown with up to 6 inches of water over the crowns; smaller *A. gramineus* is best grown with no more than a couple of inches of water over the crowns. Both species spread but aren't considered invasive, and they're safe to plant in earth-bottomed ponds. Zones 5 to 11.

*Variegated sweet flag (*Acorus calamus *'Variegatus')*

■ *Butomus umbellatus* / Flowering Rush

Description: This handsome species produces grassy clumps of dark green 2- to 3-foot-long leaves topped by attractive, spidery clusters of rose-pink flowers in summer. The narrow leaves are triangular in cross section.

Culture: Flowering rush grows in full sun to very light shade. Plant it in standing water, with up to 6 inches of water over the crowns, or in soil that is constantly moist. An ideal plant for areas with cool summers, such as the Pacific Northwest, flowering rush does not grow well where summer temperatures regularly exceed 90°F. Zones 5 to 7.

■ **Canna hybrids / Aquatic Canna**

Description: These bold plants resemble the common cannas grown in gardens everywhere. They produce clumps of large, broad leaves topped in summer by showy red, gold, yellow, salmon, or orange-spotted flower trusses. Longwood hybrid aquatic cannas are especially heavy bloomers. *Canna americanallis* var. *variegata* has stunning orange flowers and green leaves striped with yellow.

Culture: Grow aquatic cannas in full sun. They thrive in either constantly moist soil or with up to 6 inches of standing water over the top of the crowns. In Zones 7 to 11, aquatic cannas can be grown as perennials. Farther north, either grow them as annuals and buy new plants each year, or overwinter them indoors. To overwinter them, lift the containers out of the garden in fall after light frost. Cut back the tops of the plants to 6 to 8 inches and dry off the roots. Shake the soil off the roots and store in barely moist peat moss at a temperature of 45°F. Repot in spring and replant outdoors after danger of frost has passed.

Longwood hybrid aquatic cannas

■ *Colocasia* / Taro

Description: Taros are tender perennials grown as annuals in much of North America. Although their flowers are insignificant, they bear huge leaves that resemble elephant's ears in shape. They add a lush tropical look to a water garden. Use them as specimen plants or combine them with marginals that have contrasting foliage. Green taro *(C. esculenta)* is 4 or more feet tall with deep green leaves that can reach 2 feet or more in length. Violet-stemmed taro *(C. esculenta* var. *fontanesii)* bears dark green leaves that resemble green taro's on violet stems. A closely related plant, variegated taro (*Alocasia* × *amazonica* 'Hilo Beauty') bears similar lush leaves that are mottled with ivory.

Culture: Taros can be grown as perennials outdoors in Zones 9 to 11; in colder zones, they are grown as annuals and are killed by the first hard frost. *Colocasia* spp. can be grown in constantly moist soil or with up to 12 inches of standing water over the crowns of the plant. They grow in full sun to partial shade. Plant *Alocasia* × *amazonica* in full sun to very light shade. It grows in constantly moist soil or with up to 2 inches of water over the crowns of the plant. Taros can be overwintered as house plants in a sunny window. Keep the soil constantly moist or keep pots in a bucket with a few inches of water over the soil.

Green taro (C. esculenta)

Alocasia × amazonica *'Hilo Beauty'*

■ *Cyperus* spp. / Cyperus

Description: Cyperus are grown for their handsome clumps of evergreen leaves borne in umbrella-like whorls atop tall stems. Although tropical in nature, they are grown as annuals or tender perennials in areas with repeated frost. The tufts of foliage are topped in summer by sedgelike brown flower clusters. Umbrella plant or umbrella palm *(C. alternifolius)* is often sold as a houseplant. It ranges from 1 to 3 feet in height. Dwarf umbrella plant (*C. alternifolius* 'Gracillus') is a smaller version of its larger cousin that never exceeds 2 feet. Consider it for container gardens or small pools. Papyrus or Egyptian paper reed *(C. papyrus)* is a large plant that provides a dramatic accent for any garden large enough to accommodate it. Stems, up to 14 feet tall, are topped by exotic-looking moplike whorls of leaves. Dwarf papyrus (*C. isocladus,* formerly *C. haspan*) maintains a more manageable size; plants reach $2^1/_2$ feet.

Cyperus *spp.*

Culture: Grow all species of cyperus in partial to full sun or in shade, with preferably at least one hour of direct sun. In Zones 9 to 11 they are hardy perennials; grow them as annuals and replant each year in Zones 8 and north. Or treat them as tender perennials and bring them indoors in fall and move them outdoors in spring. Over winter, keep the soil constantly moist. Stand pots in a shallow pan of water or place them in a bucket and keep a few inches of water over the soil. (Keep an eye out for aphids and spider mites and control them with a soap spray such as Safer's.) Outdoors, all cyperus can be grown in constantly moist soil, and the larger species can be grown in standing water with up to 6 inches over the crown of the plant. Plant *C. alternifolius* 'Gracillus' with no more than 2 inches of water over the crown.

- *Eleocharis montevidensis* / Spike Rush

Description: Spike rushes produce clumps of narrow, grassy leaves that are round in cross section. Twelve-inch-tall *E. montevidensis* produces tiny, brown, conelike clusters of flowers at the tips of each leaf. It is native to eastern North America. Chinese water chestnut *(E. dulcis)* bears graceful 1- to 3-foot-long leaves and is grown for ornamental value as well as its edible tubers.

Culture: Plant spike rushes in full sun, although both species tolerate a site that receives as little as three hours of direct sun. Both species grow in the constantly moist soil of a bog garden or in standing water: *E. montevidensis,* Zones 6 to 11, is best grown with no more than 2 inches of water over the crown of the plant; *E. dulcis* with up to 12 inches over the crown. *E. dulcis,* hardy in Zones 7 to 11, spreads widely in earth-bottomed ponds.

- *Equisetum spp.* / Horsetails

Description: Horsetails, also called scouring rushes because of the silica contained in their stems, produce evergreen clumps of round, jointed stems that look grass- or rushlike. These primitive plants do not have leaves, although some species produce featherlike branches at the joints. Instead, the stems function as leaves. The flowers are actually spikelike, spore-bearing cones borne in summer and fall. Common scouring rush *(E. hyemale)* generally reaches about 18 inches in height, although plants can grow to as much as 4 feet tall. Dwarf scouring rush *(E. scirpoides)* grows 4 to 8 inches in height. Both species are native North American plants.

Culture: Plant horsetails in full sun or in very light shade, provided they receive at least three hours of direct sun daily. Both species spread vigorously by rhizomes and can be invasive in earth-bottomed ponds. Grow them in

*Horsetail (*Equisetum *spp.)*

soil that remains constantly moist; *E. hyemale* can be grown with up to 6 inches of water over the crown of the plant. Smaller *E. scirpoides* can be grown with 1 inch of standing water over the crown. *E. hyemale* is hardy in Zones 3 to 11; *E. scirpoides,* Zones 4 to 11.

■ *Houttuynia cordata* / **Houttuynia**

Description: Houttuynia is grown for its heart-shaped leaves rather than its flowers, which are spike-shaped and surrounded by white, petalless bracts. While the species has green leaves, 'Chameleon', sometimes sold as 'Rainbow', bears leaves that are handsomely variegated with rose-red, maroon, yellow, and cream.

Culture: Grow houttuynias in full sun to partial shade. They will perform happily in moist soil or with up to 6 inches of water over the crowns of the plants. Zones 5 to 8.

Water poppy (Hydrocleys nymphoides)

■ *Hydrocleys nymphoides* / **Water Poppy**

Description: Glossy oval leaves and cup-shaped, three-petaled flowers make water poppy a delightful addition to any water garden. The lemon yellow 2-inch flowers appear all summer long. Both flowers and some of the leaves are held slightly above the surface of the water.

Culture: Water poppy is a tender perennial that can be grown as an annual from Zone 8 north. It grows in full sun to very light shade. Plant it with 4 to 12 inches of water over the crowns of the plant. In areas where it is not hardy, replace it annually or bring in a few plants in fall and grow them in a sunny window in an aquarium or bucket with a small amount of soil in the bottom. Water poppy spreads widely and is invasive in earth-bottomed ponds if not killed by winter freezing. Zones 9 to 11.

- *Hydrocotyle verticillata* / Water Pennywort

Description: The rich green, scalloped leaves of water pennywort form a dense, 3-inch-tall mat on the water's surface in shallow-water areas. The sprawling stems send out roots along their length and root anywhere the water is shallow enough. Plants produce tiny white flowers in summer.

Culture: Grow water pennywort in full sun to partial shade. Plant in constantly moist soil or in water up to 2 inches deep. Pennywort spreads readily in earth-bottomed ponds. Zones 5 to 11.

- *Iris* spp.

Description: Irises are beloved by dryland and water gardeners alike for their spectacular flowers and handsome, strapshaped leaves. The flowers have three inner, upright petals, called standards, and three outer petals that stick out or down, called falls. Plants range from 2 to 4 feet in height. Some of the showiest irises are ideal for the shallow edges of a water garden or the constantly moist conditions of a bog garden. Siberian iris *(I. sibirica)* produces attractive clumps of leaves topped by showy blue, white, purple, violet, and yellow flowers in late spring to early summer. Many cultivars are available, including ones with bicolor blooms. Japanese irises *(I. ensata,* formerly *I. kaempferi)* have round, flat flowers with large, showy falls. Flowers come in blue, violet, white, rose-pink, and wine-red. Yellow flag *(I. pseudacorus)* bears bright yellow flowers in early summer. Two native North American species,

Louisiana Iris 'Katherine Cornay'

blue flag *(I. versicolor)* and Southern blue flag *(I. virginica)*, produce blue-violet blooms in early summer. Red iris *(I. fulva)* is another native species that features narrow leaves and red-brown to copper flowers. Gardeners in Zones 6 to 11 can grow Louisiana irises, a group of hybrids derived from several native species. Louisiana irises bloom from late spring to early summer and range in height from $1^1/_2$ or 2 feet up to 5 feet. Flowers come in purple to blue-black, sky blue, vermilion red, and violet.

Culture: Grow irises in full sun in soil that is rich in organic matter. *I. sibirica* grows in a wide range of soils, from the moist but well-drained conditions of a perennial border to the wet conditions of a bog garden with up to 2 inches of standing water over the crown of the plant. *I. ensata* requires moist to boggy soil in summer, but it does not tolerate soil that is flooded in winter. Other irises can be grown in constantly moist soil or standing water; the depth varies with the species and cultivar. *I. versicolor, I. fulva, I. virginica,* and many of the Louisiana iris cultivars can be grown with up to 6 inches of water over the crown of the plant, and *I. pseudacorus* with up to 10 inches over the crown. Divide iris clumps in summer or early fall if they become overcrowded. *I. ensata* is hardy in Zones 4 to 9; *I. sibirica,* 2 to 9; *I. pseudacorus,* 4 to 11; *I. virginica,* 7 to 11; *I. versicolor,* 2 to 8; and *I. fulva,* 5 to 11. The Louisiana hybrid irises are hardy in Zones 6 or 8 to 11, depending on the cultivar.

■ *Lysimachia nummularia* / **Creeping Jenny**

Description: Also called moneywort, this ground-covering species features creeping stems with round leaves. Plants are wide-spreading but remain between 2 and 3 inches tall. Small, bright yellow flowers appear in summer. The cultivar 'Aurea' has bright, golden yellow leaves.

Culture: Creeping Jenny grows in full sun to shade. It thrives in ordinary garden soil or can be planted in up to 2 inches of water, in which case the leaves spread out over the water's surface. Thin plantings if they spread too far. Zones 3 to 8.

- *Marsilea mutica /*
Four-Leaf Water Clover

Description: Although its common name suggests otherwise, water clover is actually a species of fern. The leaves, which resemble four-leaf clovers, float on the surface or stand just barely above it. Each set of four leaves is marked with an attractive pattern of brown and yellow. European water clover *(M. quadrifolia)* is similar but has smaller leaves that are not patterned.

Culture: Grow water clover in full sun to partial shade. Set plants with 3 to 12 inches of water over the crowns. Water clover is an enthusiastic spreader, nearly impossible to get rid of once established in earth-bottomed ponds. Thin it out as necessary to keep it contained. Zones 6 to 11.

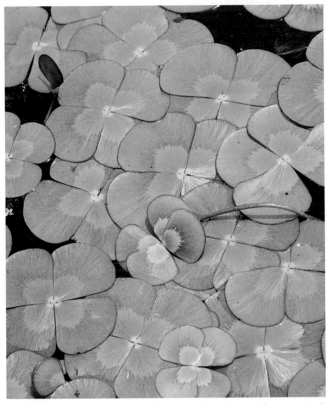

Four-leaf water clover (Marsilea mutica)

- *Mentha aquatica, M. citrata /* **Aquatic mint**

Description: This relative of common garden mints features pungent oval leaves and rounded clusters of lilac summer flowers. It reaches 3 feet when grown in moist soil but will spread across the water's surface to about 6 inches when grown in standing water.

Culture: Grow aquatic mint in full sun to partial shade, planting it in moist soil or in up to 2 inches of water. Like common garden mints, water mint is a vigorous spreader. It is also a valuable edge cover for a pond when allowed to spread. Zones 6 to 11.

■ *Myriophyllum aquatica* / **Parrot's Feather**

Description: Parrot's feather is grown for its attractive green leaves. Underwater the leaves are hairlike, but when the lank stems emerge to float on the surface or rise above it, they become dense and feathery. When plants are crowded or growing in very shallow water, stems may grow upright out of the water, rising from one to several inches.

Culture: Plant parrot's feather in a container filled with sand, as you would a submerged plant. Set the container in full sun to partial shade with 3 to 12 inches of water over the surface. Thin plants regularly to suit your design. Plants will take over earth-bottomed ponds. Zones 6 to 11.

■ *Nymphoides* / **Floating Heart, Water Snowflake**

Description: Both the foliage and flowers of these plants recommend them for any water garden. They bear small floating leaves marked with purple-brown or maroon that resemble water lily pads. White snowflake (*N. cristata*) bears tiny white flowers; yellow snowflake (*N. crenata*) and floating heart (*N. peltata*) bear yellow ones. *N. cristata* and *N. crenata* bloom from spring to fall; *N. peltata* blooms in spring and summer. Blooms, borne in abundance, each last only a day.

Yellow snowflake (Nymphoides crenata)

Culture: Plant *Nymphoides* spp. in containers with 3 inches of heavy garden soil topped by $1/2$ inch of washed gravel. Set the containers in full sun with 3 to 12 inches of water over the crown of the plant. Thin plants out as necessary to control their spread; otherwise they can cover the water's surface. Because they spread so aggressively, avoid planting in earth-bottomed ponds. *N. crenata* and *N. cristata* are hardy in Zones 7 to 11; grow them as annuals in colder zones. *N. peltata* is hardy in Zones 5 or 6 to 11.

■ *Orontium aquaticum* / Golden Club

Description: Native to bogs and pond edges in eastern North America, golden club produces unusual, white, pencil-like flowers with yellow tips in spring or early summer. The handsome, rounded 8- to 12-inch-long leaves are velvety blue-green. Leaves float on the surface when plants are grown submerged; when grown in moist soil, they reach up to 18 inches.

Culture: Golden club grows in constantly moist soil or with up to 5 inches of water over the crown of the plant. Plant them in dappled shade or on a site that receives up to 3 hours of direct sun daily. Zones 6 to 11.

■ *Peltandra virginica* / Water Arum

Description: Handsome arrowhead-shaped leaves make this North American native an excellent addition to any bog or water garden. Plants produce large, dramatic clumps of glossy, foot-long leaves on erect 2- to 3-foot stems. Small yellow flowers appear in summer.

Culture: Grow water arum in full sun to partial shade. It can be planted in constantly moist soil or with up to 6 inches of water over the crown of the plant. Although water arum produces large clumps, it does not spread excessively. Zones 5 to 9.

■ *Pontederia cordata* / Pickerel Rush

Description: This native North American wildflower produces clumps of handsome, waxy leaves topped by showy blue flower spikes from spring to early fall. A white-flowered form is also available. Plants reach 2 to 3 feet in height.

Culture: Grow pickerel rush in full sun to partial shade in a site with either constantly moist soil or standing water up to a depth of 12 inches. Plants spread widely in earth-bottomed ponds. Zones 3 to 11.

Pickerel rush (Pontederia cordata)

*Arrowhead (*Sagittaria *spp.)*

- *Sagittaria* spp. / Arrowhead

Description: Arrowheads make fine additions to pond edges and bog gardens, because of both their handsome leaves and their loose spikes of three-petaled white summer flowers. Native *S. latifolia,* commonly called duck potato or wapato, produces clumps of large arrowhead-shaped leaves that can reach 20 inches or more in length. The common names refer to the starchy, edible tubers once used for food by Native Americans. Plants average 2 feet tall but can be taller. As its common name suggests, red-stemmed sagittaria (*S. lancifolia* forma *ruminoides*) boasts bold red stems. Double arrowhead (*S. sagittifolia* 'Flore Pleno') bears spikes of round white flowers on plants up to 3 feet in height.

Culture: Grow arrowheads in full sun to partial shade. They can be planted in constantly moist soil or in standing water with up to 6 inches over the crowns. Plants can spread widely in earth-bottomed ponds. *S. latifolia* is hardy in Zones 4 to 11; *S. lancifolia,* Zones 7 to 11; and *S. sagittifolia* 'Flore Pleno', Zones 7 to 11.

■ *Saururus cernuus* / Lizard's Tail

Description: Also called water-dragon and swamp lily, this native plant is a rampant spreader that produces narrow, arching spikes of fragrant white flowers in summer. The plants, which grow from 1 to 2 feet tall, bear somewhat heart-shaped leaves.

Culture: Grow lizard's tail in full sun to partial shade in constantly moist soil or in standing water up to 6 inches over the crowns. The plants spread widely in earth-bottomed ponds. Zones 4 to 9.

Lizard's tail (Saururus cernuus)

■ *Thalia dealbata* / Thalia, hardy canna

Description: Thalia is an elegant-looking marginal plant producing bold clumps of broad, nearly 20-inch-long leaves. Clumps of foliage reach between 3 and 4 feet and sometimes more. In summer plants are topped by graceful, wandlike panicles of tiny purplish flowers that can reach 1 to 5 feet over the leaves. Red-stemmed thalia (*T. geniculata* var. *ruminoides*) is a tropical species that bears larger leaves—to 30 inches long—on attractive red stems. Plants can reach 8 to 10 feet when in bloom and have violet flowers.

Culture: Grow thalia in full sun or very light shade. Plant in constantly moist soil or in standing water with up to 12 inches over the crown of the plant. *T. dealbata* is hardy in Zones 6 to 11; *T. geniculata*, Zones 9 to 11; grow it as an annual in colder zones.

Thalia (Thalia dealbata)

Graceful cattail (Typha laxmannii)   *Common cattail* (Typha latifolia)

- *Typha* **spp. / Cattails**

Description: The tall grassy leaves and cylindrical brown flower spikes of cattails are a familiar sight along pond edges and in roadside ditches throughout the U.S. Several species make fine additions to water gardens. All spread by rhizomes to form handsome clumps. Common cattail *(T. latifolia)* reaches 7 feet in height and has $1/2$- to 1-inch-wide leaves. Narrow-leaved cattail *(T. angustifolia)* produces 7-foot-tall clumps of thin ($5/16$ inch) leaves. Graceful cattail *(T. laxmannii)* also bears narrow leaves, but reaches only about 4 feet in height. Diminutive *T. minima* is perfect for even tiny water gardens; it produces grassy clumps of 12- to 18-inch-tall leaves. Its brown seedheads are round instead of cylindrical.

Culture: Grow cattails in full sun to very light shade. *T. latifolia* and *T. angustifolia* are hardy in Zones 2 to 11, *T. laxmannii* in Zones 3 to 11. All three grow in constantly moist soil or standing water with up to 12 inches over the crown of the plant. *T. minima* is hardy in Zones 3 to 11 and grows in constantly moist soil or with up to 2 inches of standing water over the crown. Cattails are vigorous spreaders and can take over an earth-bottomed pond as deep as 3 feet.

Water Garden Companions

You're really only limited by your imagination when it comes to planting the areas immediately outside the liner of your pond. Before you plant, take a moment to examine the soil, then select plants that thrive in the existing soil. Here are some ideas to get you started.

Perennials. Mounding perennials form an attractive edging for a water garden without blocking the view of the water. Consider daylilies, sedums such as 'Autumn Joy' or 'Vera Jameson', threadleaf coreopsis *(Coreopsis verticillata),* hardy geraniums (*Geranium* spp.), and coral bells (*Heuchera* spp.), to name a few. Low-growing ornamental grasses such as *Pennisetum alopecuroides* 'Hamelin' or 'Little Bunny' are also attractive. For shady pond edges, consider hostas, epimediums (*Epimedium* spp.), lungworts (*Pulmonaria* spp.), or fringed bleeding heart *(Dicentra eximia).* Taller perennials make a fine backdrop for gardens that are generally viewed from one side, especially when combined with ornamental grasses such as miscanthus. *Miscanthus sinensis* 'Gracillimus' is attractive; *M. sinensis* 'Purpurascens' flowers in late summer and has stunning red fall color.

Shrubs and Trees. Although it's best to keep full-size trees and large shrubs well away from a water garden, some selections make happy companions. Matlike creeping junipers such as 'Bar Harbor' or 'Pancake' are attractive spilling over the edges of a water garden and will conceal its edges year-round. There are many other dwarf conifers that can provide a similar function—be sure to check height at maturity before you buy. Low-growing evergreen cotoneasters such as bearberry cotoneaster *(Cotoneaster dammeri)* or little-leaf cotoneaster *(C. microphyllus)* are also delightful edgers. Dwarf Japanese maples *(Acer palmatum),* especially weeping, cut-leaved forms, are attractive cascading over the edge of a pond. Small trees also make an effective backdrop for a pond—useful for hiding the neighbor's garage or other eyesore. Consider dwarf crab apples or cherries for this purpose, but keep them well away from the pond, ideally on the north side so they do not cast shade on the water. Underplant with ground covers.

Ground covers. Many common ground covers work beautifully as pond edgings. Consider a carpetlike mix of creeping thymes such as *T. serpyllum.* Sedums, hens-and-chicks (*Sempervivum* spp.), pinks (*Dianthus* spp.), ivy (*Hedera* spp.), myrtle or vinca *(Vinca minor),* and lilyturf (*Liriope* spp.) are also all good choices.

TROUBLESHOOTING

CONTROLLING FISH PREDATORS

Although cats take an occasional swipe at pond fish, raccoons are more effective predators; they will push plants off marginal shelves in their search for fish and snails. A water garden with nearly vertical sides and without marginal shelves provides some protection against them. A dog in the yard helps keep these nighttime marauders at bay.

You can also build "scoot houses" out of stacks of bricks or weathered cinderblocks at the bottom of the pond to give fish a place to hide when predators appear. Use thick flagstone for a roof. Or build four stacks of bricks and set a container of lotus or marginals on top. Lengths of PVC pipe or narrow chimney liners too small for raccoons but large enough for fish are a good passive defense for fish. Suspending sections of large-mesh grid 6 to 12 inches under the water's surface is also effective. Make sections of grid from wide-mesh plastic netting stretched over a frame, or by fastening together untreated pine dowels. Be sure to make the grid large enough for your largest fish to swim though easily. Covering the garden with screens or plastic netting, or rimming it with a low-voltage electric fence are other options.

Herons and other fish-eating birds are also serious pests that can empty a water garden of fish in a visit or two. Suspending sections of grid in the water, or covering the water with screens or netting are effective measures. Scarecrows, noisemakers, and mock predators work briefly, until the birds realize they won't be harmed by them.

Turtles, water snakes, and frogs also eat fish. Catch offenders in a net and relocate them — with permission — to a natural pond.

FISH PESTS, DISEASES, AND PROBLEMS

Fish are especially susceptible to pests and diseases when they are under stress; minimizing stress is the first line of defense against most fish problems. Maintaining clean, well-aerated water and avoiding sudden changes in water temperature are good defensive measures to take. If fish appear sluggish with no other signs of disease, test water pH and adjust it gradually, if necessary. (See "Testing and Treating the Water" in chapter 3.) Test kits are also available for ammonia or nitrite levels. Rock salt is a good temporary treatment for restoring vigor. (The slime layer and electrolytes are critical elements for healthy fish.) One pound of rock salt treats 100 gallons of water as a one-time treatment.

Chlorine, chlorine dioxide, and chloramine — all chemicals used to treat municipal water supplies — are extremely dangerous to fish. Chloramine does not dissipate naturally from the water and affects fish slowly. Fish left in untreated water begin to hide, stop eating, become listless, and ultimately die. Always keep a large enough supply of treatment chemicals (available from water garden dealers and many pet stores) on hand to treat the entire volume of your pond in the event that you have to change the water suddenly.

Use the following list of symptoms and treatments to treat fish. If a single fish is affected, catch it in a net and move it to an aquarium filled with water from the pond for treatment. Be sure to use an aerator and cover the aquarium with weighted-down screen or netting to prevent jumping. Water garden suppliers and pet stores carry treatments for fish. Medicated fish foods are also available; treat the fish as described below and feed with antiparasitic or antibiotic for 10 days as extra protection.

Fish gasping at surface. Insufficient oxygen in water. Using a hose with a fine spray nozzle attached to spray the water is an acceptable temporary measure. For long-term correction of the problem, add a submersible pump with a fountain or waterfall to reoxygenate the water.

If the fish also have flared-out gills, treat as for anchor worms, below.

This symptom is also caused by toxins like new, untreated water that still contains chlorine, chlorine dioxide, or chloramine. If the pool is newly filled, treat the water as described in "Testing and Treating the Water" in chapter 3.

Bloody spots near fins and tail. Anchor worms. These parasites attach themselves to fish; if you look closely, you may see the threadlike worms. Several commercial treatments are available from water garden dealers and well-stocked pet stores. For effective treatment, read the label; all require repeated treatment at specific intervals to control these pests. Also feed with antiparasitic food for 10 days.

White film over eyes. Cloudy eye. This is a fungus disease that can be treated with a reliable fungus treatment. Follow the package directions, and use two treatments at the specified intervals. Feed with an antibiotic food for 10 days.

Tail and fins look rotted. Fin-and-tail rot. This is a fungus disease. Use the same treatment as for cloudy eye, above.

Furry, cottony growths on fish, especially on tail and/or fins. Fungus growths. These growths on fish are usually a secondary disease. Treat fish as for cloudy eye or anchor worm, above.

Small white spots on fish. Ich. This condition is caused by a parasite. Infected fish look as if they were sprinkled with salt. Treat as for anchor worms, but apply treatment daily for 3 to 5 days.

Large sores on undersides of fish. Furunculosis. This is a fungus disease that generally attacks fish when water temperatures are 50° to 60°F and the fish are stressed. Treat as for cloudy eye, above. Determine the cause of stress and eliminate the cause.

Fish rubbing on pots and other objects in pond. Lice. This condition is caused by parasites. Treat as for anchor worm.

Flared-out scales. Dropsy. This is a noncontagious condition that still cannot be effectively treated. Treatment as for cloudy eye may bring relief.

Fish cannot swim properly. Swim bladder disease. This is a noncontagious condition that still cannot be effectively treated. Treatment as for cloudy eye may bring relief.

Plant Pests

Caterpillars chew holes in leaves of water lilies and other aquatic plants. Control by hand picking them, or simply washing them into the pool with a strong spray of water; they will become a tasty snack for the fish. Aphids sometimes infest water lilies as well. To remove them, briskly shake affected pads under the water. Wandering tunnels in the upper surface of lily pads indicate infestation by false leaf-mining midges. Pick off and discard infested leaves as soon as you see them. Also pick off and discard leaves with black spots, which indicate fungus diseases.

Plant Predators

A variety of animals eat or disrupt plants. Raccoons tip containers off marginal shelves in their search for fish and pests. See "Controlling Fish Predators" above for suggestions on controlling them. Ducks, geese, and swans will pull up plants, especially in newly planted gardens. Protect new plantings with plastic netting until plants are established. Crawfish and turtles damage plants as well. Catch offenders in a net and relocate them — with permission — to a natural pond. Koi and other fish over 8 inches in length will dig up water lilies and other plants. To prevent this, cover the soil surface with gravel and small rocks. See "Fish for a Water Garden" in chapter 3 for another remedy.

Pond Leaks

To search out a leak, first stop the pump that cycles water through a waterfall or filter and fill up the pool. If the water level stops dropping, the leak is in the waterfall or the recirculating system. Check tubing and other connectors and tighten them. Also check the edges of the liner and pack soil and rocks back in against places where the edges are low enough to let water leak out. If the leak isn't in the waterfall or recirculating system, the water level will continue to drop, stopping when it reaches the level of the leak. If you have difficulty finding the leak when the level stops dropping, add an inch of water (remember to treat for chlorine, etc.), then drop vegetable dye into the water every foot or two near the edge. Water exiting the liner draws the dye to the leak. One place that pools leak is along the edges, where the liner has settled. In this case, also fill in behind the liner with soil and/or stones to raise the top edge. Holes in the liner can be patched; purchase patching materials for the type of liner you have and follow the package directions.

Excess Pool Debris Buildup

Several steps help prevent debris buildup, and thus the need to clean out the pool. Keep leaves out of the pool by building away from deciduous trees, stretching netting over the water in fall, and skimming off floating leaves. A Leaf Eater will suck debris off the bottom of the pool, or you can physically net it out. Finally, using bacteria and enzyme products like Muckbuster helps dispose of waste.

PHOTO CREDITS

HARDINESS ZONE MAP

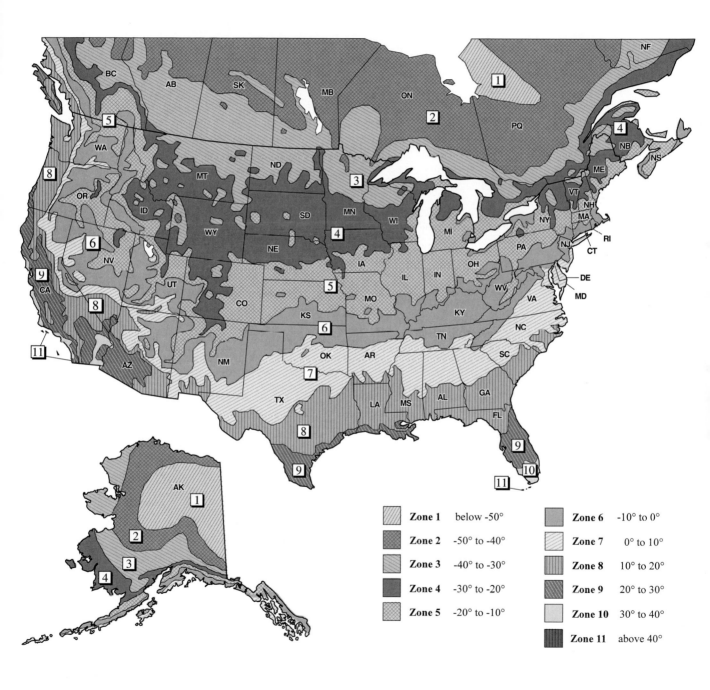

	Zone 1	below -50°		Zone 6	-10° to 0°
	Zone 2	-50° to -40°		Zone 7	0° to 10°
	Zone 3	-40° to -30°		Zone 8	10° to 20°
	Zone 4	-30° to -20°		Zone 9	20° to 30°
	Zone 5	-20° to -10°		Zone 10	30° to 40°
				Zone 11	above 40°

INDEX

Page numbers in *italics* refer to illustrations.

Titles available in the Taylor's Weekend Gardening Guides series:

Organic Pest and Disease Control	$12.95
Safe and Easy Lawn Care	12.95
Window Boxes	12.95
Attracting Birds and Butterflies	12.95
Water Gardens	12.95
Easy, Practical Pruning	12.95

At your bookstore or by calling 1-800-225-3362

Prices subject to change without notice